THE SCIENCE
OF GETTING RICH

endorsements

"Ryan is awesome! He will engage and inspire your audience with his creative superpowers."

*- **Jim Kwik**, best-selling author of Limitless, high performance memory coach & founder of Kwik Learning*

"In the years I've known Ryan, I've watched his life and career flourish as he has adopted and cultivated a wealthy mindset. He is proof that you can develop this mindset through relentless practice, humility and putting yourself out there. He has an uncanny ability to give people hope and inspire action without abandoning realism."

*- **Marissa Brassfield**, founder of Ridiculously Efficient, Inc.*

"Ryan is one of the most driven, inspired, & creative people that I have come across. His keen eye and strong desire to always learn and better his craft makes him someone that I would recommend in a heartbeat."

*- **Rick Frishman**, best-selling author, publisher & business consultant*

"Ryan is bold but humble. He is very talented in creating living online communities that learn, act and fellowship. With his keen eye for detail and outside-the-box-thinking, he has managed to connect people from around the world and unite them around common values. He genuinely cares for people and has a heart towards helping them reach their potential."

*- **Christoffer Björkskog**, programmer and systems development analyst*

"The time I spent with Ryan in planning my film fest and developing my brand was so valuable. He is really good at what he does and I'm a believer."

*- **Aman Segal**, producer & founder of Ojai Short Film Fest*

endorsements

"Ryan is one of the most creative minds I know of. He is full of impeccable integrity and excellent interpersonal skills. If you need brilliant help fleshing out your ideas or if you have a message to share with the world and need to give it wings, he's your man. I give him my highest recommendation."

- Mark Paulson, web & software developer

"There are an overwhelming number of ways to build a genuine audience and customer base. Working with Ryan has consistently helped me discard the noise and distill down the truly helpful information that's unique to my platform. He takes out the confusion and distraction, leaving you with clear and achievable steps. Brilliant."

- Leslie Calderoni, author & speaker

"Ryan is obsessed with making his clients look amazing and stand out from the crowd. He is a freaking genius. His out-of-the-box thinking, natural enthusiasm, and expertise on media strategies are among the many assets he brings to every client relationship while keeping your end goals in sight. If you want your company to stand out, talk to Ryan. His work and his integrity are top notch!"

- Jennifer Hofmann, author, business advisor & activist

"Ryan is one of the few leaders I know whose core values cause him to push others towards innovation while rolling with the punches. He is an empowering leader with the tenacity to take risks and ask tough questions that get you to think.

As someone who has worked for and with Ryan, I have the utmost respect for his work ethic and integrity. I cannot say this enough: there are few leaders that know how to invest in those they lead – and Ryan does this very well. He knows how to help people unlock their own potential in the most personal of ways."

- Cordell Winrow, fitness trainer and consultant

THE SCIENCE OF GETTING RICH

how to manifest + monetize your ideas

by Wallace Wattles
+ Ryan J. Rhoades

(2022 edition)

NEW YORK

LONDON • NASHVILLE • MELBOURNE • VANCOUVER

THE SCIENCE OF GETTING RICH
how to manifest + monetize your ideas

Published in New York, New York, by Morgan James Publishing. Morgan James is a trademark of Morgan James, LLC. www.MorganJamesPublishing.com

This book is for informational purposes only and is not intended to provide legal, accounting, medical, or other professional advice. If you require legal advice or other expert assistance, make sure to seek the services of a professional. Also, we disclaim any liability from actions you may take after reading this book and do not claim to be special gurus or anything of that sort. In a nutshell, we make no guarantees as to any particulars regarding income, wealth, or results that you may or may not see from reading this.

The publisher has made every effort to ensure accurate information, web addresses, and contact information at the time of publishing. However, we assume no responsibility for errors or changes that occur after publication. If you do find errors, please contact the author and we will do our best to update the book for future editions.

Compiled, translation, commentary, cover, & interior book design by Ryan J. Rhoades. Original publication by Wallace Wattles is in the public domain. Some pronouns and content edits have been made to make communication of core principles clearer to a modern audience while preserving the spirit of the original author's message

Proudly distributed by Ingram Publisher Services.

Morgan James BOGO™

A **FREE** ebook edition is available for you or a friend with the purchase of this print book.

_____

CLEARLY SIGN YOUR NAME ABOVE

Instructions to claim your free ebook edition:
1. Visit MorganJamesBOGO.com
2. Sign your name CLEARLY in the space above
3. Complete the form and submit a photo of this entire page
4. You or your friend can download the ebook to your preferred device

ISBN 9781631955044 paperback
ISBN 9781631955051 ebook
Library of Congress Control Number: 2021930915

Cover and Interior Design by:
Ryan Rhoades

Morgan James is a proud partner of Habitat for Humanity Peninsula and Greater Williamsburg. Partners in building since 2006.

Get involved today! Visit MorganJamesPublishing.com/giving-back

table of contents

You never change things by fighting the existing reality.

To change something, you have to build a new model that makes the existing model obsolete.

Never forget that you are one of a kind. Never forget that if there weren't any need for you in all your uniqueness to be on this earth, you wouldn't be here in the first place.

And never forget, no matter how overwhelming life's challenges and problems seem to be, that one person can make a difference in this world.

In fact, it is always because of one person that all the changes that matter in the world come about.

Be that one person.

R. Buckminster Fuller
(July 12, 1895 – July 1, 1983)

You are the reason that I create.

My team and I could not do what we do without the love and support of countless people from all around the world.

If you are reading this right now, then you are one of those people. Thank you.

You have helped us build a life around what we love and the pursuit of our ideas, our art, and our creativity. For that, we cannot thank you enough.

Your value and self-worth is not defined by the fluctuating numbers in your bank account, how much or how hard you work, the color of your skin, what political party, gender, or religious group you identify with, your sexual orientation, where you're from, or how many shares of stock you hold. You get to **decide what you're worth** regardless of all of that.

You have within you the power to bring creative solutions to all kinds of problems, big and small.

It is my hope that this book helps you along that path. It has done so for me. This is for you, your family, your friends, and your tribe.

I wish you evermore abundance, peace, joy, love, hope, creativity, empathy, and inspiration all the days of your life.

Thanks for joining us on this journey so far. Keep creating.

If you let your learning lead to knowledge, you become a fool.

If you let your learning lead to action, you become wealthy.

– Jim Rohn –

foreword by
Marissa Brassfield

As I write this, we are in the midst of a war on creativity and ambition.

2020 was a doozy: a global pandemic, raging wildfires, civil unrest, polarizing political elections, economic uncertainty, and the deaths of cultural icons. Every day, we fight to stay motivated, focused, productive and fulfilled despite a tsunami of negative news and misinformation that overwhelms our consciousness, hijacks our brains, and triggers our "fight, flight, or freeze" responses.

We're treading water in a noxious primordial soup of distraction, confusion, disorder and uncertainty. We're searching for direction and not finding it in the usual places. Trust in the government, media, the economy, education, and our financial system is at an all-time low. We don't know who to trust – and worse yet – we don't know whether the information we're viewing can be trusted.

We are at the precipice of major cultural, societal, and economic shifts...and those shifts will require upgrades in the way we view the world and the opportunities around us.

How can you focus on making things better when it seems like the world around you is collapsing?

It's a challenging environment to carve out space and time to think...much less create, innovate and design something new. *Yet that is **exactly** what we must do right now.*

The truth is that the information that barrages us rarely affects our immediate environment and daily lives. It is by and large algorithmically chosen to drive consumption behavior and feelings like fear, greed, outrage, righteousness, and division…all while delivering big profits and power to those who benefit from cultivating the chaos.

The skills we need to heal from the past and build a future that is better than our present are empathy, creativity, collaboration, ingenuity and hope.

This book was written for times like these, and I'd like to invite you on a journey towards reinventing yourself and the world around you. A lot of people believe you can't be rich and create true art. It's the myth of the starving artist: the idea that there's no money in creativity, and that to be wealthy, you need to compromise your values or integrity *(or at least have a rich family)*. **Those are the old rules.**

Today, everyday people – and yes, that means you – have the tools and technologies at your fingertips to transform ideas into self-made fortunes. With the power of the internet and by connecting creators with consumers and vendors, you can come up with a product idea or start a company in a day, launch in a weekend, and fulfill orders within a week. So the question remains...*why aren't we all rich entrepreneurs?*

The truth is that wealth is a mindset.

...and it's much scarier and riskier to put our ideas out into the public for criticism than it is to put in time at a "normal" job. Humans evolved as tribal creatures, wired to resist doing something different out of fear of being excommunicated, shunned or rejected by the community. For thousands of years, this wiring has worked in our favor. Our amygdala – an ancient portion of our brain associated with our "fight, flight or freeze" response – once helped humans evade predators.

In modern life, though, our amygdala often hinders more than it helps. Blame that on algorithm-driven news feeds with fear-mongering headlines, combined with a productivity-driven work culture that aims to turn employees into fleshy robots who **consume instead of create**... and never quite get far enough ahead to escape the matrix.

No wonder it's so hard to come up with a breakthrough business idea or a plan for financial freedom. It's not your fault. And there is hope if you want to get off the hamster wheel. But you have to let go of one thing first...and that is the false idea that wealth is just tied to *doing*. What do I mean by that? A wealthy mindset isn't about doing, it's about being. What you do is a result of your sense of who you are and your core values. A wealthy mindset sees collaboration and opportunity instead of competition and obstacles.

A wealthy mindset plays win-win games where all parties benefit, rather than zero-sum games, where someone has to lose for another to succeed.

A wealthy mindset protects sovereignty and resists encroachment or manipulation from external forces. A wealthy mindset is fit: agile, adaptable, constantly improving, and well-practiced. In the years I've known Ryan Rhoades, I've watched his life and career flourish as he has adopted and cultivated a wealthy mindset. He is proof that you can develop this mindset through relentless practice, humility and putting yourself out there.

Ryan has an uncanny ability to give people hope and inspire action without abandoning realism. His creative endeavors and the connections he builds are a product of this. In this book, you'll find the tools, strategies, and most importantly – the mindsets you need to get focused and stay inspired so you can reclaim sovereignty over your life by paying a lot more attention to how you think, act, and interact with the world than you do by staring at a screen all day.

So much of what's going on out there is meant to shame you into silence and scare you into playing small instead of aiming for the stars. You don't have to listen to that noise. Invest the time to digest this book. Revisit it again and again. What you'll read in these pages can change your life if you let it. **The world needs you.**

We need your voice, your creativity and your ingenuity. Are you ready? Let's go.

Marissa Brassfield
Founder, Ridiculously Efficient, Inc.
Los Angeles, CA

making something out of nothing
some background, some context, and an introduction by Ryan J. Rhoades

"When you grow up, you tend to get told the world is the way it is and your life is just to live your life inside the world. Try not to bash into the walls too much. Try to have a nice family, have fun, save a little money. That's a very limited life.

Life can be much broader once you discover one simple fact: Everything around you that you call life was made up by people that were no smarter than you.

You can change it, you can influence it, and you can build your own things that other people can use.

Once you learn that, you'll never be the same again."

- Steve Jobs (1955 - 2011)

Your realization of the principle above can completely transform your life. I don't just say that to be dramatic. I say it because I know that it has transformed mine. I stumbled upon a tattered old version of this book at a thrift shop in 2014 for 99 cents. I had just moved to a new city and was clueless and paralyzed with fear over how I was going to make ends meet. I was a broke, in-debt small business owner with no customers or income in sight. The ideas and perspectives in this book helped me turn my finances around while learning the art of creativity and how to make something out of nothing. It's taken me years of practice, struggle, frustration, almost insane amounts of reading, work, research, and lots of trial and error, but the fact that you are reading this right now is proof of the principles within.

As a longtime writer, designer and multimedia producer, one of the things that I have always been fascinated by is the ability for people to envision something in their minds and then – through some sort of mental, physical, or technological sorcery – create the very thing that they had imagined.

Our minds are like powerful supercomputers in many ways. If you can learn to harness yours and tune out *(or at the very least turn down)* the noise and chatter that can so often fill it, you too will start to experience the never-ending excitement that can come from the act of leaning into your own creativity and the flow state that comes with it. That is just one of the things you will begin to experience and understand how to harness as you read through this simple but powerful book. But before we get into all of that, I first would like to share a bit more background to lay the foundation for what you're about to read.

When I was a kid, I spent a lot of time in my aunt and uncle's print shop. In the late 1980's and early 1990's, computers were just starting to show up in people's homes, and they had started their own printing business. They had some of the first computers I had ever seen and it never ceased to amaze me to watch something that once only existed within the screen come to life when sent to the printing press. My mother was a public school teacher, so we eventually got access to one of the early Macintosh computers. I remember one of the first things I did was look for ways to draw digital pictures on a blank digital canvas. There was a particular digital painting program that got my attention. *(A quick shout out to all the public school teachers...you deserve a massive raise and better benefits for all the hard work you do. Organize and make it happen!)*

One of my first digital creations was a fake movie poster depicting some terrified earthworms fleeing from a giant beak fishing around in the soil. There were no colors in the monitor, so everything we did at that time was in black and white. I drew ragged-looking, giant block letters with the mouse and wrote the title of my imaginary movie: *BEAK* — and I was hooked. I printed it out and was fascinated by the fact that I had just done some sort of digital wizardry and now was holding something that had once only existed in my imagination. Of course there were sequels – *BEAK II: Revenge, BEAK Returns,* and countless more. As time went on and the technology improved, we were introduced to color screens. Each installment of these digital creations got more and more detailed, with more earthworms meeting their untimely demise in the mouth of this imaginary digital bird that was never fully revealed *(primarily because anytime I tried drawing a whole bird, it looked so ridiculous that I couldn't bring myself to show it to anyone).*

2

Eventually, we started using some greeting card production programs; one of them was called Print Shop Pro. We would design and print out our own greeting cards and give them to family members for holidays, birthdays, etc. I also would occasionally write short stories, print them out and staple them together, making my own little books. I spent a lot of time tinkering around with the software, looking for any way that I could to take what I was imagining and turn it into something tangible. I made buttons, signs, magnets, t-shirts...all kinds of things. Every time I made something new, I would find ways to make it better the next time.

I was very fortunate to have parents who cultivated and encouraged this kind of creative pursuit in me. I was always given the freedom to draw, or build, or play with toys that would give me some kind of blank canvas to work with like LEGO's, the Etch-a-Sketch, or Lincoln Logs. This made a huge impact on creating things out of nothing and just having fun with different ideas. **Play is key to seeing success in any creative endeavor.**

If you are a parent, I can't recommend enough that you constantly encourage the creative pursuits of your children.

Music, art, writing, architecture, 3D design, filmmaking, dancing, painting...all forms of creative expression will help them better understand themselves and the world around them. It will empower them to learn to work with their imagination to create amazing products and experiences for themselves and others, for which they can later learn to charge a pretty penny. If you couldn't tell from my *BEAK* story, I also grew up watching a lot of cheesy sci-fi and monster movies like *Godzilla, Jason and the Argonauts, Gremlins, Jaws*, etc.

In the same way that I was fascinated by the creations my aunt and uncle would make in their print shop and the things we were able to make with our Macintosh at home, it blew my mind that people could take clay, plaster, or other materials and create imaginary monsters for movie heroes to fight against. This was well before the era of computer generated images (CGI), but still *I was hooked*. My dad and I would often stay up late into the night watching the behind-the-scenes videos of how the movie magic happened. I learned all about green screens, claymation, and puppets...and then watched a bunch of adults do a lot of fun things that I didn't often see anyone doing anywhere other than on the TV. It made me want to learn everything I could about movie makeup, special effects, and film.

4

Eventually, all I knew was that I wanted to figure out how I could make a living having fun and making cool ideas come to life.

The seed of that concept showed up early for me, but it is only now probably 25 years later that I am realizing how much of that time spent cultivating my creativity has led me to where I am now. My team and I have worked with amazing people from all over the planet through the magic of the internet. The things that we are now able to create with the various technologies that are available to us is just mind blowing. It is my hope that you start recognizing and capitalizing on this fact...and that you do so in an empathetic, compassionate, and sustainable way as a force for good and a better future.

It is an amazing thing that some of the financially "poorest" people in some regions of the world now have access to information, education, opportunities, and abilities that even the kings and queens of the earth couldn't imagine just 50 years ago. I have a dear friend in Nigeria who has built an amazing design business for himself out of nothing. He has clients all over the world now. I even helped him publish his first book! *(It's called From Me to You by Dotun Fadairo)* You can communicate with someone on the other side of the world instantaneously with a video call through a number of methods. It's the closest thing to teleportation that we've currently got, people. That's awesome! You can immediately find the answer to just about any question *(or at least start yourself on the right track)* at the speed of thought just by doing a few simple internet searches from your phone. **That is game-changing.** A lot of people who have grown up with the world like this don't yet realize the power to create that is well within their grasp and quite literally at their fingertips. I aim to change that. If you really want to change your life for the better, learning how to use your technology as a *creative tool* versus a *consumption device* is a great place to start. *(For more on that, check out Cal Newport's excellent book Digital Minimalism)*

Looking back, all of these things have had a huge impact on my life and career choices. I still make my own products, creations, and designs come to life, now more than ever. I am blessed to be able to do what I love and actually get paid well for it. It has taken a great deal of time and effort in order to be able to say that, and a big part of it is learning to recognize the value and worth that your creativity can bring to the marketplace.

For example, in our home, the majority of the coffee mugs that we have are our own designs. Most of the t-shirts and hooded sweatshirts that I wear are our own styles. The posters hung up in our creative studio and a lot of the artwork around our home is our own work as well. We don't do this to be narcissistic or self-congratulatory. We do these things as a constant reminder that we really CAN create the world we want to live in and to surround ourselves with things that encourage us to always pursue what we love and the betterment of our craft.

As I mentioned earlier, I stumbled upon *The Science of Getting Rich* in a thrift store in early 2014. At the time, I was struggling financially in some pretty intense ways which I'll talk about more later. I didn't even know where my rent money was going to come from. Over the years, my wife and I have had a number of difficult struggles to overcome and oftentimes when I am feeling stuck, I go browsing through old books in thrift shops or in my public library. Upon initially glancing through Wallace's little book, I have to admit that I scoffed at a lot of it.

"How could there be a SCIENCE to getting RICH?" I wondered. I was really skeptical, especially since I was coming from a place where I had very little money in the bank at the time. Even still, the author seemed very insistent that his methods would work, and, well…I was desperate for something to get me out of the hole we were in. So, I spent the 99 cents, brought it home, and started reading it.

The language in it was hard to get through at times. There were plenty of instances where I struggled through it because it felt so ridiculous, especially when my bank account was draining, we weren't finding any new clients, and I didn't know how I was going to pay my bills…but something about it kept me reading.

Maybe it was the certainty with which the author wrote. Maybe it was the fact that I was at a place where I needed to make something happen so badly that I was willing to try anything. Whatever it was, I'm glad that I did. Once I finally started realizing that the author was mostly referring to the creative process when he talked about what he calls "The Certain Way," a bunch of things started clicking into place for me.

The creative process in general has always been something that has captivated my attention. A big part of my life's work *(and I believe my life's purpose)* is to help others harness their own creativity and empower people into a life of more freedom and creative expression.

We have published books, created entire product lines *(which you can check out at RDShop.biz)*, built businesses, created marketing campaigns, hosted events, planned parties, consulted with business owners and non-profits, raised money for charity, made countless flyers and business cards, built websites, released music albums *(soundcloud.com/ReformDesigns)*, held art shows, started podcasts, and countless other "creative" things - **but what they all have in common is that the first step is having an idea.**

The first step is dreaming up the concept. It could start with just a fleeting thought flashing through your subconscious - whether in the form of a mental image or a word or a song playing somewhere in our mind. It could be different for you, but what really matters is what you *do* with it.

The whole creative process starts like a seed.

Bringing ideas to life is easier when you think of your ideas like seeds, and your canvas like soil. The time and energy you spend tending to that soil *(working on your canvas)* acts like water and sunlight that causes that seed to grow. Eventually, the seed will come to fruition and your ideas will come to life as you learn to better harness your creativity and your craft...but you need to make sure that the seed is in an environment where it can grow and flourish.

A big part of that for me boils down to making sure that I have intentionally created space for my creative pursuits. If you want to learn how to play an instrument, for example - don't leave it in your closet or your basement. Get it out and put it somewhere that you'll see it every day. The same goes for writing or any other type of creative art. It's on *you* to cultivate the space for your creativity to grow... so start there if you don't know where to start. Start by clearing space - mentally and physically in your home - for you to do your creative work every day.

Throughout the book, you will see the author repeatedly refer to what he calls "formless substance."

Over the years I have interpreted that phrase as any kind of blank canvas: physical, digital, metaphysical, or otherwise.

A blank piece of paper. An empty room or a blank wall. A blinking cursor on an empty screen. A lump of clay. A new relationship. A green screen. A blank sheet of music. A napkin in a restaurant. Even empty space in the cosmos. You get the idea.

These things *(and many others that I'm sure you could now think of)* are all "formless substances" until acted upon by you and your imagination. As you read, if you feel yourself getting confused, try to slow down and write down what you're stuck on or what is causing you to feel stuck, then keep reading and come back to the question later. You may find it is answered as you continue along. I know that was the case for me.

I would highly encourage note-taking and doodling as you go along. Write some notes to yourself in a new notebook or in the margins *(or if you're reading this on a digital device, take some notes on that)*. I've also included pages for note taking at the end of the book in the appendix. I am sharing this work with you because I wanted to help breathe fresh life and a bit of my own commentary into something that has made a big difference in my creative and business pursuits over the years.

I have found that the philosophies and suggestions within it have enabled me to think more creatively and critically about problems that I am facing. Rather than looking to outside sources for help, it has helped me instead to begin looking inward and working to figure out creative ways to fix things or make something new.

Creativity is not something that I ever encourage rushing, unless you are trying to simply get better at creating what you imagine faster for the sake of improving your own craft. Treat it like a fun game you're playing, not a test you're trying to pass or to try and win some external award or approval. This book has helped me in a number of ways, not the least of which is the almost constant reminder to give myself the grace to embrace the creative process and trust that as long as I just keep working at something, eventually I'll see it come to life.

Spending a little bit of time on your creative or business pursuits every day is a great way to see major progress over time. This is a much easier process when you have crafted and built an environment in your home or workplace that lets you quickly get into the creative zone / flow state.

You may have picked this up because you were looking for a way to make money and you certainly can use it that way - but for me, and I believe for Mr. Wattles as well – being rich isn't just about how much money you have in the bank.

Being rich is about being content with what you have and learning how to find that contentment with what's right in front of you. It's about leaning into the process of creativity and tapping into the power that is within you to make something of value.

Being rich is being able to manifest the very things that you are wanting to create in order to make the world a better place than you found it. This is about, as author Seth Godin says, how to "make things better by making better things."

I have found more than anything that this book has helped me figure out more practical ways to harness my own creativity and make something out of nothing. There is nothing quite like holding something in your hands that once only existed in your imagination or on a digital screen. I hope that this book and my commentary on it helps you in the realization of your goals and dreams. I have formatted it in a way that I hope is easy to digest and with plenty of room for you to take your own notes at the end.

As I've said before and will say again, I in no way claim perfection or that I am some special guru with special knowledge. I just read a lot and try stuff to see what works. Trial and error is the essence of the scientific method, right? The wisdom I have gleaned from the books I have read has so positively impacted my life and I am grateful to be able to do my best to condense some of the lessons I feel that I've learned from others who have come before me with you. What you choose to do with what you learn here is your decision alone.

We all have made mistakes and have regrets, but one thing that I have *never* regretted is any time that I have spent cultivating my creativity or my ability to make the things I once could only imagine. I have never regretted any time I have spent reading books on subjects that interest me and that inspire me to be better today than I was yesterday. I have read and revisited this book again and again - not always from cover to cover, but often times I will pick it up when I am feeling stuck, frustrated, or can't figure out the answer to a creative problem I am trying to solve. I have found that it has been a great resource to keep within reach. The perspectives and advice in it have helped me more times than I can count. I wish the same for you.

If you have never had anyone give you permission or encouragement to pursue your creativity, live your dreams, paint that picture, take that course, learn that language, write that book, or play that instrument - let this be it.

Don't wait for some mystical sign. Learn to re-embrace the child-likeness and imagination required to fully excel in any creative or business pursuit. It takes time, but I assure you that it is worth it. This book can help you not just with practical matters, but with spiritual, emotional, and mental matters as well. It also has been very helpful for me in navigating the extreme uncertainty of the times in which we live, as I have recognized that the struggles that we all face in this life can often be overcome if we look to those who have gone before us for clues on how to proceed. Frankly, I don't know much about Wallace's own personal financial success while he was alive, but I do know his work has helped me with my own.

Tom Butler-Bowdon says of Mr. Wattles' background:

> *"In 1890's and 1900's America, many people felt oppressed by a system where great industrial trusts and extremely wealthy individuals held sway. [We have many rich] capitalists of our age, but in relative terms, most of them did not match the wealth of Rockefeller and Carnegie in their time.*
>
> *In a more brutal economic era without safety nets, the average person clung onto jobs they hated or kept up businesses that weren't doing well for fear of slipping through the cracks entirely. From a poor rural family himself, Wallace Delois Wattles would not have escaped such fears."*

If you are reading this and are working at creating a better life for you and your loved ones...or maybe you are just feeling down, frustrated and hopeless about your own financial situation, know this: **I get it.** I'm not writing this while sitting pretty on my third yacht in the Caribbean. I'm writing this as someone who is building every day and working to create value, products and services for the world around me. I'm saying this as someone who, at the time of this writing, still has a substantial amount of student loan debt that can often feel like I'll never pay off. However, I felt that same way about my credit card debt when I first read the book you now hold in your hands. That debt now is completely paid off.

Financial freedom starts first in your mind and with the way that you look at the world around you. This book will help with that first step and many more. I can definitely say I am much "richer" now than I was when I first came across this book from a financial standpoint and beyond. It isn't because there is some magical, mystical, ethereal and unknowable thing you have to figure out in order to see more "riches" come to you. It isn't about just sitting around hoping for some secret knowledge to drop out of the sky and into your lap. You don't need to have been born into a rich family. In fact, I think in some ways people who are born "rich" in the traditional sense often have a disadvantage to the kinds of riches we're going to talk about in this book.

That's because the first step to really being "rich" is recognizing the wealth that is already yours and being thankful for what you do have, right where you are.

Once you start with gratitude, creativity flows naturally...and from there comes an infinite number of ideas that you can use to create wealth and a better life for you and your loved ones. The amount of work that is required to really see lasting personal and professional change is not something that a lot of people are too keen to talk about. That kind of decision forces you to come face to face with the cold, hard reality of whatever situation you may be dealing with.

You might be facing a mountain of debt or troubles - from medical bills, student loans, credit cards, child support payments, poor financial decisions from when you were younger, mortgage payments, relationship or family drama, etc.

Whatever the cause or the crisis is doesn't matter. What you will find as you work through the material in this book and test out the concepts for yourself is that no matter what you are dealing with, you are ultimately the one who is in control of how you respond to the situations you're facing and what you build.

You can always learn. You can always get better. You can always improve. You can always practice. You can make the *decision* to get stronger and smarter. The practice is the point. You can choose to stop waiting to be "picked." You can choose to share your voice, your story, and your art. And you should. The rewards are worth it, which will include the connections and things you make along the way.

When you stop trying to "arrive" somewhere, you are immediately free to just create.

At some point, with practice, experience, patience, and after more hours than you can count *(because you've stopped counting)*, you will look around and realize how far you have come. You will see in more ways than you could have once imagined that you have arrived at the goals you set for yourself. If you don't set those goals first and start working towards them, they're just never going to happen. Yes, every single day. Yes, even when you don't feel like it. It's really that simple.

So what are you waiting for? An invitation? Here you go. Consider this one.

I INVITE YOU TO PLAY THE CREATOR GAME. There are no winners or losers – only creators. Do you accept?

Here's the thing: you don't need anyone's permission or invitation to be a creator. You already are one. You just have to decide what you're going to do about that. You have permission to make your art and share your voice. More than that, you have a RIGHT to. Remember this – any new endeavor takes time and practice. Lots, and lots, and lots of practice. This journey is about creating a life that you don't want to escape from. It's about building something of value that you believe in. It's about looking forward to getting up in the morning so you can keep building.

That might sound like a radical and impossible idea to you right now. That's okay. Just let yourself imagine what it might feel like to experience a life like that. Give yourself the grace and permission to explore different and new ideas. Thank you for reading. I wish you well on the path. This is the way. ;-)

Here we go, champ.

You are cordially invited to begin
building a better, richer, more
fulfilling and creative life that
you don't want to escape from.

Right here, right now.

This is the first step. Repeat the following out
loud & sign at the X...but only if you mean it!
(or at least want to mean it)

*I refuse to allow my current life and financial results to influence
my thinking. I have a power within me that is far superior to all
conditions and circumstances that I ever will encounter. I am
choosing to learn how to unlock and unleash my own creativity and
build a better life for myself and my loved ones. I choose right here
and now to commit to this creative journey and focus on what I can
do here and now. I choose to build. **I choose to be a creator.***

X _____   date: _____

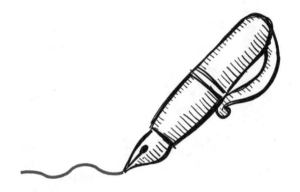

Fun fact:

The affirmation you just signed on the previous page is an updated version of one that I made myself when I first started reading The Science of Getting Rich in 2014.

9/8/14

I refuse to allow my current financial results to INFLUENCE my thinking.
    I have a power within me that is far superior to all conditions + circumstances that I ever will encounter.

Awesome! Now, just a few more things before we get started...

When I first read this book, I was broke, desperate, and didn't know how I was going to buy groceries that week. I know what financial struggle feels like and what it can do to your mental state, your health, your work, and your relationships. Money is a tough issue to wrestle with, and it's not one that many of us are ever properly educated on...let alone how to make money with your creativity. That is one of the main reasons why I am publishing a new edition of the book that you are holding – to simplify some things that, once harnessed, will empower you to new heights of creativity and success.

I believe the principles in this book can help get you through your financial struggles, and challenges. I know that they have helped my family and I do so. What you also may find, as I did, is that **poverty is not just a financial thing.** It all starts with how you think and the stories you choose to believe about yourself and your current circumstances...and *you can change all of those things.* I have always been intrigued by creativity in general - and I found that this book gave me a better understanding of how to harness and prosper from the creative process.

Spoiler alert: it always starts out messy and almost certainly will take longer than you want it to. Just accept that now and you'll be ahead of the game.

Also, if you grew up in any kind of organized religion or church system like I did, I can pretty much guarantee that there will be certain phrases or ideas in this book that may make you uncomfortable and maybe even a bit angry. At the very least, you'll probably be tempted to put it down and tell yourself that it's just "another one of those prosperity gospel, name-it and claim-it books." If you do feel that way, I simply ask that you push through it. You may be incredibly skeptical of anything that you find labeled as "self-help" or "how to get rich" in a book store or in a library. That's fine – I was too. I struggled with a lot of these things the first few times I read this book. *Who did this Wallace Wattles guy think he was, anyway?* But I had to let that go. I was desperate to make something happen, so I kept reading. What kept me going was my fascination and curiosity over how the author talked about the creative process and how to go about harnessing it in a way that CREATED wealth instead of looking for ways to EARN it.

A huge part of making ideas happen starts with visualizing the goals you want to achieve, writing down what you imagine, and – most importantly – **taking action to bring the vision to life.** You will *never* have all the steps laid out right in front of you – but you almost always can figure out what the *next* step is. As you read, you will see this theme repeatedly mentioned in a variety of ways. I have found that it is primarily through regular practice, repetition and discipline that we grow to be better at anything we do. *(This isn't rocket science of course, but how much of that realization do we regularly apply to our lives and business endeavors? Probably worth meditating on that a bit...)*

Most times, the hardest part can be just getting started.

We must learn to rest and lean into the present moment. It is only there that we can cultivate curiosity and focus on creativity like when we were younger and less distracted or cynical about the world around us. This is largely about using your imagination on purpose instead of being so reactive to everything everyone else wants you to react to. Now that you're all grown up with a fancy *(or a terrible)* job, property taxes *(or renter's insurance)*, or maybe even some important sounding letters after your name *(and a boat load of debt)*, you very well may have forgotten how to access that childlike imagination.

Allow me to propose to you right from the start that this quite possibly may be the reason that you're feeling stuck and frustrated with your life or business. *(I assume you are feeling stuck at some level, otherwise you probably wouldn't be reading this book!)* My goal - and the original author's goal, I believe - is to help you tap into your imagination again in order to solve your problems with your creativity...and in a way that generates a sustainable income for you and your family. Don't misunderstand as you go through it – he is in no way *(as far as I can tell)* insinuating that you should simply sit around daydreaming. Of course not! Nothing would ever get done.

He is saying that your imagination plays a huge part in the creative process. He's saying that you should spend your energy focusing on the things you can change, what you can make, and the things you can do rather than getting caught up with distractions and fear about all of the things that are outside of your control. We'll continue to repeat these things throughout the book to hammer the point home.

You'll see a lot of encouragement to **always do what you can, with what you have, where you are.** The vast majority of any "success" that we have had in our lives and business endeavors hinges solely on this concept. If you grew up in church, the concept of "stewardship" should sound familiar to you. I believe a lot of what the author references throughout the book is along those lines.

For example, you may want to learn how to play the piano but might not have one. You may love the feeling of the weighted keys, and the amazing sound produced by a grand piano, but you also may not have the room for one, let alone the finances to afford it. What you **can** do, however, is download any number of free or inexpensive software programs or apps on your phone, tablet or computer and learn how to play on a digital version in the meantime. *(GarageBand is a great place to start if you use Apple products. If not, just look around online for free or open source digital music programs and tutorials.)*

You could also *(as I did)* keep an eye open at different thrift shops around your city; quite frequently you will find used or even new musical instruments for very cheap. Additionally, there are often people giving away and selling musical instruments used or lightly used in local online marketplaces like Craigslist, Facebook, etc. I taught myself how to play the piano with a keyboard that normally was $150. I found it in great condition for $30 at the same local thrift store where I purchased my first copy of the book you're about to read. The keyboard even lit up when I played it! *(Yes, I'm a geek.)* It took me about ten years of regular practice and intentional learning and playing with music instruments and software, but I am now at a point where I own a much higher quality instrument. It is one that I know how to use much better because I worked with what I had available instead of the constant pursuit of *more*. We all can struggle with wanting something to be perfect before we are willing or ready to get started. *(Let's clear this up early: you'll never feel ready. Just get started!)*

A huge part of all of this is learning to recognize and seize opportunities that others frequently overlook or miss.

If you decide to try this out in the music arena, for example, don't be surprised if other people start noticing and think of you as they come across instruments that someone is giving away or selling for cheap, especially as you grow in your skills and continue practicing some new art form.

I know a number of people that this has happened to just in my own immediate family, but it certainly doesn't happen overnight! All of that said, **I do not claim to believe or adhere to every principle or idea that Wallace Wattles** *(the original author)* **presents in this book.**

There are a number of things that I simply don't agree with for any number of reasons, and I am quite sure that you will find the same to be true for you. Choose to focus on and work with the principles that resonate and make sense for you, and you'll do just fine. Don't get caught up on the rest. There are a number of concepts in this book that I have found to be quite true in practice and with large amounts of testing over time. That is what "science" boils down to, anyway, right?

My goal in publishing this is not for the sake of trying to tell you what to think or believe. It is to offer insight and ideas that I have found to be practical and helpful for me and my family in times of crisis.

I have wasted a lot of time debating uselessly about religion and politics over the years and have found much more joy and peace when I choose to accept the fact that life is an ever-changing and ever-evolving dance of ideas, concepts, beliefs, successes, failures, and pursuits...and that in a whole lot of ways, *none of us know what on earth we're doing and we're all figuring this journey out as we go along.* I'm not sure about you, but I know that I feel a lot better when my focus is on doing what I can to make the world around me a better place instead of wasting my limited time and energy trying to wrap my head around the complex nuances of global politics, giving myself panic attacks by binging on "news," and speculating 24/7 about a never-ending media-manufactured tsunami of crises that I have no control over. I *definitely* feel better when I choose to stop caring so much about what everyone else is thinking or doing and get to work taking action and making stuff.

As a personal rule, I work very intentionally to not to be as dogmatic as I used to be about a lot of different things. It is far too stressful to try and fulfill the insatiable and unattainable goal of trying to be right all the time. I don't claim to be *good at* not still getting agitated about things outside my control...just that I'm aware it's not a good idea and I'm working on it. :)

I don't claim for one second to be the authority on "getting rich" – at least not in a financial sense or based on how much money I have in my bank account compared to a whole lot of other people on this floating blue rock we call Earth. I'm pretty sure that Jeff Bezos made more money in the thirty seconds it took me to write this paragraph than I made all year so far...but I also have no desire whatsoever to be that financially rich. More money – especially at those levels – often does just lead to more problems. I don't know about you, but I'm not interested in that. If you are, this book probably isn't the one for you. Otherwise, if you are interested in learning ways to create and develop your own definition of wealth for yourself and your loved ones, then you, my friend, are exactly who I wrote this for. My goal here is not to try and "get rich" by publishing a book about getting rich *(bruh...so meta)*. I am putting this out there because I believe the message within it is more important than ever as our planet is collectively facing some very real and intense challenges. We need innovators and creative thinkers with fresh solutions to help fix this mess we're all in. We need builders, artists, learners, and creators everywhere to come together.

We don't need more bureaucracy, fear-based reactive thinking, gossip, drama, or distractions.

We need stillness. We need empathy. We need imagination. We need people like you to discover and unleash your creative superpowers.

We need the insights that develop within the place of present-moment focus and intention. We need action. This book is about cultivating and *choosing to do* those things. I am so immensely grateful for the work that others have done in compiling their wisdom and insights for navigating the uncertainties of our collective existence in books. Their work has helped keep me sane in a world that can often feel like it has gone crazy. I've spent well over a decade studying and learning everything I could about entrepreneurship and making ideas happen. I don't say that to boast - I say it to give you context for what you are about to read. I have done my best to condense the insights I've learned and put into practice over the years into practical, actionable steps you can take *today* to start turning your life around. Just so you know, at the time of this writing, I have plenty of concerns about cash-flow and paying my bills just like you do. Maybe less, maybe even more, but it doesn't matter. *What matters is that we're on the same team here, champ.*

I'm not sure those concerns ever completely go away...but at this point in my life, I'd much rather focus on learning how to handle the situations life throws at all of us and still thrive despite them instead of just complaining all the time. If we let ourselves slow down long enough, we can find our way through any challenge we face. The perspective we choose to take in any given circumstance will determine how well or how quickly we solve a problem. This book is designed to help you shift your perspective on what "being rich" means for you and those around you.

The goal here is to help you live a more fulfilling, more expressive and rich life...on your terms.

This particular volume has been one of a number of books I've read that has helped me realize the riches that I do have *(food, water, shelter, family, friends, freedom to create)* while continuing to build a life of ever-increasing abundance. It has helped me learn how to focus on being thankful for what I have, rather than constantly seeking more just for the sake of having more. It has helped me to realize the utter uselessness of getting caught up in whatever crisis the outside world and the for-profit "news" media is currently panicking about...and to focus instead on my own sphere of control and influence. It has helped me to focus on channeling my creative energies into what I can make in the pursuit of making things better. *(For additional reading recommendations on this topic and more, make check out the back of the book. I'll keep reminding you about them. They're good.)*

Being rich is not about the constant pursuit of more material or cash-based wealth as much as it is about being content with and working with what you have...which will always lead to more expansion.

If you gave Leonardo Da Vinci a crappy paintbrush, chances are he'd still paint a pretty good piece of art even without the most expensive brushes on the market. **It's not about the tools.** It's about the artist, how they choose to use their imagination, and the time and attention spent learning the craft. The tools are simply a medium for the artist to express themselves. Sure, everyone wants to have the best tools available - but I have found over the years that if I get stuck on that, I don't create. If I focus on being thankful for what I **do** have and what I **can** use, I am easily able to shift into "the zone" and start making the things I have set out to make.

For me, *The Science of Getting Rich* isn't so much THE absolute "how-to" manual *(as the author states or heavily implies a few times)* - but it certainly is **A** how-to manual in a vast sea of others that can help you along your journey of creative discovery. My hope is that you will find the perspectives presented in this book helpful in understanding how to unlock and harness the creative process in a way that helps you bring more wealth into your life.

I believe that if you choose to take this path that it can bring you into a life of excitement, adventure and abundance that you previously would not have thought possible. I say this because I know that it has done so for me. I go back and reread it regularly and hope that you will as well. I wish you abundance, joy, wisdom, more creative ideas than you know what to do with, and the freedom to explore all that which makes you come alive. Cheers to you and your pursuit of making the world a better place through your creativity!

A quick logistical note about my commentary

I have added my own thoughts at certain points throughout this edition. You'll see a line separator with the science beaker icon like you see here to indicate where my commentary begins and another line break to indicate where it stops. Sometimes it is short like this, and other times I go into more depth at the end of the chapters. Wallace Wattles' original version was admittedly hard for me to get through in some places and he says some things I simply don't agree with. I have done my best with this new edition to provide context, clarity, and commentary in areas that I struggled to understand or when disclaimers are needed. To make communicating the core message of the book simpler for today's audience, I have also updated the original text in ways that better capture what I believe was the essence of Wattles' message while removing some things that I felt distracted from the core principles. Thank you for reading. I appreciate and believe in you!

So why should you care & what the heck is "formless substance" anyway?

Let's set this up right from the start – this journey that we are all on is really, really intense. I'm not going to dance around that. Times are tough and most of us have all endured staggering and varying levels of trauma – individually and collectively. It can feel like the only thing we know for sure is that there's a whole lot we don't know for sure. My hope is that this book will help you refocus on what you *can* do and create a better life for yourself despite the noise and chaos.

As I have been working on the 2022 edition of this book, our planet is in the midst of all kinds of converging crises. There is a mind-boggling level of division around a whole host of issues – global and local. Economies are failing. Businesses large and small are closing their doors, some for good. Political differences and misunderstandings are driving families and friends apart while giant old school media and business monopolies rake in record profits...all at the expense of our collective well-being. Our planet's climate emergency hangs over us all. *(Yes, I'm one of **those** people who believe that we should be doing a whole lot more to create cleaner, better energy solutions that don't destroy the planet for profit-and-power-thank-you-very-much).*

There is uncertainty everywhere about just about everything...and in a whole lot of ways, nobody knows what in the world to do to fix it.

Pandemics. Wildfires. Ice storms. Racism. Oppression and civil unrest around the world. Hurricanes. Earthquakes. Wars. Rumors of wars. Global protests against authoritarian regimes, crony surveillance capitalism, and police brutality. Betrayals. Political division unlike most of us have ever experienced. Panic. Fear. Deception. Propaganda. Corruption. Misinformation. Attempted insurrections. Neo-nazis marching in the streets with...I'm sorry, wait a second...are those *Tiki Torches?*

Yikes. Can someone try turning the simulation off and turning it back on again? I think somebody is drunk at the wheel.

It sure can seem like as a species that we are having some serious issues getting our act together...let alone even trying to come to an agreement around any sense of objective reality. I don't know about you, but even finding the motivation to get out of bed in the morning or eat three meals a day has been much harder to do lately. We are bombarded at every turn and on every screen with notifications, distractions, crises, trauma, and things that scream for our attention. It sucks. And it's enough to make anyone – regardless of your religious or political affiliation – feel like everything's gone crazy. I get it. In many ways, it has. The systems that so many of us have grown to rely on for most of our lives are failing in spectacular, unexpected, and rage-inducing ways. The notion of returning to the "normal" that we were all used to before 2020 is pretty much a fantasy.

We can't (and shouldn't) go back to how things were before 2020.

Not gonna happen. No point even lying to ourselves and acting like it will. We have all been enduring sustained, long-term traumas of various types and severities just in 2020 alone, and as a species we're going to have to figure out how to heal and rebuild after that. I'm not talking about some woo-woo hyper spiritual or tech utopia BS here. I'm talking about us having the courage to move on from our collective BS and *build something better right where we are.*

What we can (and must) do is figure out what we're going to create in the wake of 2020 and its aftermath. That's why I'm releasing this book now. I'm a designer and an artist by trade - and I have seen first hand time and again the peace, the prosperity, the excitement and the enjoyment that comes from leaning into your own creativity. That is one of my wishes for you as you go through this book: that you discover and unlock the riches already within you and use those riches to build something better than we've been able to so far. It's not because I think I have all of these world-saving ideas or that I think I'm some better-than-you guru trying to make a quick buck by selling a book and hosting another conference. I was fed up with boring "networking" meetings and video chats *before* 2020.

I don't know very much for certain...but one thing I do know is that we aren't going to fix the problems that we face as a planet and a species with the same modes of thinking that got us into this mess in the first place. Stay with me here...because I've got some theories and principles to share with you that are designed to help you navigate the chaos and uncertainty of it all.

It starts with you realizing that you have within you the power to create positive change right where you are...with what you already have and what you already know.

This book isn't about just making money. It is about how to make something out of nothing and create order out of chaos. It is about how you can monetize what you create and in so doing, how you will find a type of riches that cannot be obtained through the typical *(and tired)* cutthroat business models that are so prevalent today. If you ask anyone who has obtained significant amounts of wealth, the likelihood is very high that they'll tell you what appears to be a universal principle.

You will never feel successful or rich if you are constantly pursuing more of something just for the sake of more.

You will only find sustainable success and riches when you choose to be thankful with what you have right now, focus on the present moment instead of fantasizing or worrying about the future, and utilize what is at your disposal to build for the next steps for your journey. Yes, this is a choice.

It is a daily practice. It is not a place that you arrive at. You will live a successful life when you make it a priority to live each day in a way that feels like a success to *you* – and that means having to get clearer with yourself about how you define success and what your priorities are.

This book is a lot more about shifting your perspective and looking within yourself to cultivate the riches that are waiting to develop in your life than it is about how to build a more robust stock portfolio or getting into the glorified gambling that is day-trading. I'm not interested in that.

What I am interested in is figuring out how we as creators, builders, artists, and entrepreneurs can come together and *build something better*.

ESPECIALLY if you don't think you're any of those things, stick around. This book is for you – but we'll get into that more soon. It is not lost on me that I am releasing a book about "getting rich" during some really insane and challenging economic times. We'll get to that, too. There are overwhelming cultural and societal issues that we are all facing and there's probably at least a little part of you that thought the title of this book sounded like a gimmick or a scam. It is not. I promise you - there is no shortcut here to the kind of "success" that we will explore in this book together. It is going to take work, and it will not be easy.

If easy is what you are looking for, let me just save you the time right now: You are looking in the wrong place.

If, however, you're looking for creative solutions that can help you weather the storms of uncertainty that this life will throw at you, I invite you to continue reading. I am relatively sure that critiques of this work would come from those who may question how financially "rich" I am at the time of publication, so let's get that out of the way. Suffice it to say that my financial situation is much better today than it was during the last major financial crisis in 2008...and I attribute much of that success to the principles that I discuss in the pages you are about to read, the mentors, friends and family who have helped me along the way, and the books, practices, and resources that I recommend throughout.

My interest is not in debating the nuances of those details. Your results may certainly vary, but it is worth noting that Wallace Wattles' original version of *The Science of Getting Rich* was published in 1910, and since then has been acknowledged by many around the world as a huge inspiration and guide for cultivating a richer life and healthier perspective on the world around us.

Let me make it plain right from the start: I do not define "rich" in simply financial terms. "Rich" is a subjective word that we will unpack together in this book, and each one of us has the privilege of deciding what a "rich life" looks like for us. This book focuses primarily around issues of your world view and the mindsets that can help you develop more abundance and creativity in your life.

I am not an economics guru or a professor and I do not claim for one second to be the foremost authority on how to maximize your investment profits or how to make a million dollars in a year. I'm not interested in playing status games.

If you want additional practical tools and direct tips on balancing your books, mastering your credit, and really diving deep into practical financial logistics, make sure to pick up a copy of Ramit Sethi's excellent book, *I Will Teach You to Be Rich*. It is an indispensable addition to any library if you want to continue getting better at managing and mastering your finances. That all said, let's dive in here with a simple but powerful concept...

Creativity always starts out messy, unformed, and chaotic.

Throughout this work, the original author mentions the phrase "formless substance" repeatedly. So why should you care about that? Quite simply: it is the foundational concept upon which you can build the solutions to just about every problem and crisis you may ever face. Now go back and read that again. "Formless substance" can be viewed as any type of blank or unfinished artistic or creative medium. In all of my experiments with a variety of art forms over the last several decades, I find that they all share a similar characteristic. They all start blank...*formless*...void. Waiting for someone to come along with a bit of ingenuity, some imagination, and maybe a little bit of bravado and the desire to make something new.

Examples could include a new canvas from the art store, an empty notebook or sketchbook, a blank piece of sheet music, a lump of clay, the interior of an empty room, a blank website template, or even a dish you are preparing for a meal. Even your world view is formless when you show up on this crazy blue rock. What you feed your mind on and what you create informs how you see the world over time. Don't make it complicated - this can be as simple as a blank piece of paper. What the original author is talking about really just boils down to anything that requires your imagination, some time, and focused intentional energy to take form. I believe you can even apply the same concepts to the relationships in your life - as all relationships require molding, feedback, patience, communication, attention, and imagination to keep them healthy and vibrant.

When you work at all of these things over time, you will ultimately create that which you envision if you apply your energy and focus towards building that vision.

In releasing this new edition of *The Science of Getting Rich* during these very tumultuous, scary, and uncertain times, my goal is primarily this: that you stop getting distracted by the millions of things outside of your control that scream for your attention and instead learn to look within yourself for creative solutions to the problems that you are currently facing. There is no way I would be able to focus long enough to release this new edition if I was not intentionally pulling away from all of the crises and distractions in "the news," on the internet, and the myriad of things that so many of us can get caught up in.

Creativity comes from a place of rest.

If you're constantly subjecting yourself to trauma, fear, and the ad-driven for-profit distraction algorithm echo chambers that we call social media, it's no wonder so many of us are burnt out, anxious, depressed, and exhausted. This new edition of the book only exists because I chose to self-publish the first edition back in 2018. The work that goes into writing, publishing, and then marketing a book is more than I ever thought it would be...but the journey has produced incredible results for me and my team. The work is worth it. A couple of years after having the self-published edition out on the market, I was approached and offered a publishing deal with a New York based publishing house...during a global pandemic, while millions of people lost their jobs, their healthcare, and their economic security.

When so many others were struggling, I was offered an amazing deal. I am humbled by the opportunity to share this new edition with you and I am not naive to the privilege of being able to do so when things are so difficult for countless others. My hope is that this book helps you and those around you the way that it has helped me navigate *(and sometimes even thrive)* during crisis. Years and years of struggle, practice, trial, and error is the only path I know to any of the "success" that I have in my life. I'll get more into the details of how this edition came about later, but just know that I wasn't born into a "rich" family, and nobody gave me a multi-million dollar loan to start any of my business or creative endeavors.

I just like to try new things and tinker around until something works. It's not glamorous, but I can promise you that I am living a much "richer" life as a result of the principles that you're about to dive into than I ever thought possible when I first came across this book. If you've got a story or an idea within you, put in the work and get it out there. The tools are already at your fingertips. **You just need to get started...each and every day.**

It will take time, but eventually the right people notice and doors can open for you that you previously had never imagined. I started my creative journey with a crappy laptop and a cardboard box because I couldn't afford a real desk. Let's just say I have a better creative studio today than I did then...but here's the key again, said in a different way:

Everything starts with a blank page or an empty canvas. Formless and without shape.

Every world changing idea, every book, every poem, every new piece of artwork starts at the same place: with curiosity and possibility. It begins at the place where "the way things are" suddenly becomes "the way things could be." The first step to unlocking your creativity is choosing to cultivate your own curiosity. You have to be curious enough about whatever ideas or thoughts are going through your head in order to process and act upon them. It starts when you decide to ignore the way things have been done before and choose to forge a new path beyond the well-worn trails. It all starts with a decision to put your pen to the blank page, your brush to the canvas, or when you decide to start tapping away at the keys or playing around on that instrument.

Creativity is not something that just falls out of the heavens and bestows upon you a brand new thing or successful idea. Creativity is the process by which you strengthen yourself, develop your ideas, and sharpen your skills through repetition, practice, and more practice. Growing up in a world of microwaves, 3D printers, TV-and-music-and-messages-and-movies-and-games-on-demand, we have been conditioned to expect things instantaneously. Try asking people how much they love patience and watch them cringe. On the flip side, I'm learning to appreciate the process...because it works.

I'm learning to love how creative all of us are and can be if we make the choice to continue working at it every day. The next time you feel discouraged about whatever it is that you create or are working towards creating, remember that it all starts blank. Formless. You must merely begin, day in and day out. This is about cultivating a daily practice – not arriving at a destination or seeking some high or feeling. That's how everything that once was formless begins to take shape.

One step, one idea, one brush stroke, one note, or one word at a time.

Action is the antidote to despair.

- Joan Baez -

introduction by Wallace Wattles

This book is a practical manual, not a study of theories. It is intended for the people whose most pressing need is for money - for those who wish to get rich first, and discuss theories later.

It is for those who have, so far, found neither the time, the means, nor the opportunity to go deeply into the study of metaphysics. It is for those who want results and are willing to take the conclusions of science as a basis for action, without going into all the processes by which those conclusions were reached. It is expected that the reader will take the fundamental statements upon faith, just as you would take statements concerning a law of electrical action if they were stated by a Marconi or an Edison. If you take the statements by faith and act upon them, you will prove their truth without fear or hesitation. For the benefit, however, of those who wish to investigate philosophical theories and so secure a logical basis for faith, I will here cite certain authorities.

The theory that one substance manifests itself as the seeming many elements of the material world is an old idea that has been around for ages. It is the foundation of many different philosophies like those of Descartes, Spinoza, Leibnitz, Schopenhauer, Hegel, and Emerson. The reader who wants to dig into the philosophical foundations of this is advised to read Hegel and Emerson for themselves. The plan of action that I share here was arrived at from the conclusions of philosophy and study. It has been thoroughly tested, and bears the supreme test of practical experiment: it works. If you wish to know how the conclusions were arrived at, read the writings of the authors mentioned above. If you wish to reap the fruits of their philosophies in actual practice, read this book and do exactly as it tells you to do.

**- Wallace D. Wattles
(1860 - 1911)**

Obligatory disclaimer ahead!

The original author of this work is very confident of his methods, as you can and will continue to see. I will likewise keep mentioning that it is best for you to try things out and see what works for you, rather than 'doing exactly as [he] tells you to do'. I can't (and won't) promise specifics on results that you'll see by taking action on the principles you are about to dive into. There is no need to stress yourself out or do anything stupid if something doesn't seem to be working for you. Try something else!

Remember that the essence of the scientific method is trial and error. Recognize that and apply it to your financial and creative endeavors. As it pertains to taking the author's word on faith, you have to decide for yourself what works for you, what doesn't, and assess the risks involved in doing so. I do not make so bold a claim as Wattles does as it pertains to finances, but I know for sure that much of what is in this book has helped me make a great deal of money over time. Take that for what it's worth.

Don't burn yourself out by spending a bunch of energy trying to make sure you're right all the time. A huge part of the creative process as well as the "science of getting rich," is – as I understand it – about taking your time and trying new things even if at first they may seem out of your comfort zone. You can then scale up the things that are working well. This is a simple concept, but it is certainly not "easy."

We live in an age when distraction can come at us from any direction, and it's more important than ever to be able to focus on what is truly important if you want to see your goals and dreams come to life. You are the only one who can decide how to define that. For additional reading recommendations that will help expand on the practicality of some of the philosophies in this book, look into the writings of the Stoics like Marcus Aurelius and Epictetus as well as those in the back of this book. It boils down to focusing on what you can control and taking action there.

Success usually comes to those who are too busy to be looking for it.

- Henry David Thoreau -

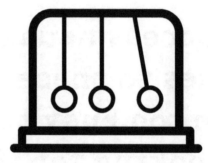

chapter 1:
the right to be rich

Whatever may be said in praise of poverty, the fact remains that it is not possible to live a really complete or successful life unless one is rich.

No person can rise to their greatest possible height in talent or soul development unless they have plenty of money. To unfold the soul and to develop talent, you must have many things to use, and you cannot have these things unless you have money to buy them with.

People develop in mind, soul, and body by making use of things, and society is so organized that humanity must have money in order to become the possessor of things. Therefore, the basis of all advancement for humanity must be the science of getting rich.

The object of all life is development. Everything that lives has an inalienable right to all the development it is capable of attaining.

Your right to life means the right to have the free and unrestricted use of all the things which may be necessary to obtain your fullest mental, spiritual, and physical development.

In other words, your right to be rich.

In this book, I shall not speak of riches merely in a figurative way; to be really rich does not mean to be satisfied or contented with only the bare minimum.

No person ought to be satisfied with a little if they are capable of using and enjoying more. This is not to downplay gratitude for what you have - that is important, but we will get to that later. The purpose of nature is the advancement and unfoldment of life.

Every person should have all that can contribute to the power, elegance, beauty, and richness of their life.

The person who owns all they want for the living of all the life they are capable of living is rich, and whether we like it or not, no one can have all that they want without plenty of money.

It is better then to accept this reality than to fight it, and figure out how to create that wealth in your own life.

Life has advanced so far and become so complex that even the most ordinary man or woman requires a great amount of wealth in order to live in a manner that even approaches completeness.

Every person naturally wants to become all that they are capable of becoming — this desire to realize innate possibilities is inherent in human nature; we cannot help wanting to be all that we can be.

Success in life is found in becoming what you want to be. You can become what you want to be only by making use of things, and you can have the free use of things only as you become rich enough to buy them.

To understand the science of getting rich is therefore among the most essential of all knowledge.

There is nothing wrong in wanting to get rich. The desire for riches is really the desire for a richer, fuller, and more abundant life - and that desire is praiseworthy.

The individual who does not desire to live more abundantly is not common *(or is lying to themselves)*. Those who do not desire to have money enough to buy all they want is out of the ordinary indeed.

There are three motives for which we live:

- ## We live for the body

- ## We live for the mind

- ## We live for the soul

No one of these is better or holier than the other - all of these are desirable, and no one of the three - body, mind, or soul - can live fully if either of the others is cut short of full life and expression.

It is not right or noble to live only for the soul and deny mind or body. It is wrong to live for the intellect and deny body or soul.

We are all acquainted with the loathsome consequences of living for the body and denying both mind and soul. We see that real life means the complete expression of all that someone can give forth through body, mind, and soul.

No individual can be completely happy or satisfied unless their body is thriving fully in every function with the same being true of their mind and soul.

Wherever there is unexpressed possibility or function not performed, there is unsatisfied desire.

Desire is possibility seeking expression, or function seeking performance.

You cannot live fully in your body without good food, comfortable clothing, warm shelter, and freedom from excessive toil. Rest and recreation are necessary to live a healthy, fulfilled life.

You cannot live fully in your mind without books (and time to study them), opportunity for travel and observation, or without intellectual companionship.

To live fully in mind you must have intellectual recreations, and you must surround yourself with all the objects of art and beauty that you are capable of using and appreciating.

To live fully in soul, you must have love, and love is denied expression by poverty. A person's highest happiness is often found in the bestowal of gifts on those they love.

Love finds its most natural and spontaneous expression in giving.

The person who has nothing to give cannot thrive and be successful in their place as a husband/father, wife/mother, or citizen of their community and country. It is in the use of material things that you find full life for your body, develop your mind, and unfold your soul. It is therefore of supreme importance to you that you should learn how to create your own riches.

It is perfectly normal and right that you should desire to be rich. If you are a living, breathing person, you cannot help doing so. It is perfectly right that you should give your focused attention to the science of getting rich, for it is among the noblest and most necessary of all studies if you want to truly live a fulfilled life and achieve your goals.

There is a big difference between pursuing financial well-being because you know it is necessary for you to thrive and pursuing riches because you are greedy and self-serving. One will lead to fulfillment and the latter will lead to ruin.

You can render to God and humanity no greater service than to make the most of yourself. Don't short-change yourself or believe the lie that you are not good enough. You can become good at anything that you put your mind and energy into.

Some of my own thoughts here...

One of the most difficult hurdles for me to overcome has been this initial piece - the 'right' to be rich. The more I meditated on it though, I started to see the truth in what Wattles shared.

The author is trying to convey that it is very difficult, if not impossible, to do all of the things that you want to do in your life if you do not have the financial means to do so.

If you just stop and think about this, you should find that it is merely a statement of fact, not a personal attack on your character, your beliefs, or anything of that sort. We all have basic physical, mental, and emotional needs – and if any of these are withheld, there is much suffering. More often than not, the reason for those sufferings boils down to the lack of finances.

The goal here is not to think that more money in and of itself will make you happy. The point is to realize that by creating more sustainable income for yourself and your loved ones that you will have more freedom, options, and time to do the kinds of things that do make you happy.

There is nothing wrong with wanting that kind of freedom. Everyone does. *Don't suppress it. Embrace it. Just make sure to do so in a way that leaves you feeling fulfilled and excited instead of full of unnecessary negativity around making more money for yourself from a place of greed or fear.*

This will take time, but it is worth it.

Success consists of going from failure to failure with no loss of enthusiasm.

– Winston Churchill –

chapter 2:
there is a science
of getting rich

There is a science of getting rich, and it is an exact science, like algebra or arithmetic.

There are certain laws which govern the process of acquiring riches. Once these laws are learned and obeyed by any person, they will get rich with mathematical certainty.

The ownership of money and property comes as a result of doing things in a certain way. Those who do things in this certain way, whether on purpose or accidentally, get rich - while those who do not do things in this certain way, no matter how hard they work or how able they are, remain poor.

It is a natural law that like causes always produce like effects. Therefore, any man or woman who learns to do things in a certain way will get rich.

That the above statement is true is shown by the following facts:

Getting rich is not a matter of environment.

If it were, all the people in certain neighborhoods would become wealthy. The people of one city would all be rich, while those of other towns would all be poor, or the inhabitants of one state would roll in wealth, while those of an adjoining state would be in poverty.

Everywhere we see rich and poor living side by side, in the same environment, and often engaged in the same vocations.

When two people are in the same locality, or in the same business, and one gets rich while the other remains poor, it shows that getting rich is not – *primarily* – a matter of environment. Some environments may be more favorable than others, but when two people in the same business are in the same neighborhood, and one gets rich while the other fails, it indicates that getting rich is the result of doing things in a certain way. The ability to do things in this certain way is not due solely to the possession of talent, for many people who have great talent remain poor, while others who have very little talent get rich.

Studying the people who have gotten rich, we find that they are an average lot in all respects, having no greater talents and abilities than other people. It is evident that they do not get rich because they possess talents and abilities that other people don't have, but *because they happen to do things in a certain way.*

*Exclusions may apply

Obviously, I am not naive to the fact that there are people who are born into extreme, abject poverty and in very dire situations that dramatically affect their financial state as well as their well-being. There is widespread systemic poverty around the world and we all have a lot of work to do if we want to make things better for future generations.

At the same time, neither am I unaware of those who are born into almost obscene levels of generational wealth that they mismanage and abuse. Let's avoid getting caught up in extremes and outliers for the purposes of this discussion and focus on what is right in front of us and what we can do.

What I believe the author is getting at is that there are certain principles of the creative process and learning how to add value to the marketplace that will work regardless of your environment or circumstances that you are born into.

Getting rich is not the result of saving, or thrift. Many very thrifty people are poor, while free spenders often get rich.

Nor is getting rich due to doing things which others fail to do. Two people in the same business often do almost exactly the same things, and one gets rich while the other remains poor or becomes bankrupt.

From all these things, we must come to the conclusion that *getting rich is the result of doing things in a certain way.*

If getting rich is the result of doing things in a certain way, and if like causes always produce like effects, then any man or woman who can do things in that way can become rich, and the whole matter is brought within the domain of exact science.

The question arises here, whether this "certain way" may be so difficult that only a few may understand, act upon, and follow it. This cannot be true so far as natural ability is concerned. Talented people get rich, and talentless people get rich. Intellectually brilliant people get rich, and very stupid people get rich. Physically strong people get rich, and weak and sickly people get rich.

Some degree of ability to think and understand is, of course, essential - but as far as natural ability is concerned, any man or woman who has sense enough to read and understand these words can certainly get rich. Also, we have seen that it is not a matter of environment. Location counts for something - one would not go to the heart of the Sahara and expect to do successful business.

Getting rich involves the art of and the necessity of working with people, and of being where there are people to collaborate with.

If these people are inclined to collaborate in the way you want to collaborate, so much the better. But that is about as far as environment matters in this case. You can create wealth where you are. If anybody else in your town can get rich, so can you - and if anybody else in your state can get rich, so can you. *Again, it is not a matter of choosing some particular business or profession.*

People get rich in *every* business, and in every profession, while their next door neighbors in the same vocation remain in poverty. It is true that you will do best in a business which you like. If you have certain talents which are well developed, you will do best in a business which calls for the exercise of those talents.

Also, in general, you will do best in a business which is suited to your environment and location. An ice-cream parlor would do better in a warm climate than in Antarctica, and an ice fishing business will succeed better in Alaska than in Florida. Aside from these general limitations, getting rich is not dependent upon your engaging in some particular business, but upon your learning to do things in a certain way.

If you are now in business, and anybody else in your area is getting rich in the same business, while you are not getting rich, it is because you are not doing things in the same way that the other person is doing them. No one is prevented from getting rich by lack of capital. True, as you get capital, the increase becomes more easy and rapid, but one who has capital is already rich, and does not need to consider how to become so. Every business starts somewhere - and very few start with all of the financial means to accomplish all of their goals at the start.

No matter how poor you may be, if you begin to do things in a certain way, you will begin to get rich and you will begin to have capital. The getting of capital is a part of the process of getting rich, and it is a part of the result which invariably follows the doing of things in a certain way.

You may be the poorest person on the continent, and be deeply in debt. You may have neither friends, influence, nor resources, but if you begin to do things in a certain way, you must infallibly begin to get rich, for like causes must produce like effects. If you have no capital, you can get capital. If you are in the wrong business, you can get into the right business. If you are in the wrong location, you can make a change and go somewhere else.

You can do so by beginning in your present business and in your present location by doing things in the certain way which causes success.

There are actions you can take NOW to move forward and your work is to discover and do those things.

This is the Way.

If you're reading this and feeling frustrated so far because the author keeps harping on about "a certain way" and you are asking yourself, "Yeah, yeah, but what IS that certain way?" – just keep reading. **A lot of what this boils down to is your mindset and what you do with the time and resources that you already have at your disposal.**

If, for example, you are spending inordinate amounts of time binging on Netflix/ TV, mindlessly browsing the internet/social media, or engaging in other activities that will not actually lead to you producing a profit of any kind – chances are you aren't "acting in the certain way" that will lead to the kind of wealth you may want. This isn't rocket science, of course - but really ask yourself...how are you stewarding the time, resources and skills that you have? What are you learning? What are you DOING?

I would add to this section that a simple way to think about this is to **do everything you can with what you have where you are instead of focusing on the constant pursuit of more.** *An excellent book on that specific topic is "Getting Everything You Can Out of All You've Got" by Jay Abraham.*

Well done is better than well said.

- Benjamin Franklin -

chapter 3:
is opportunity
monopolized?

No individual is kept poor because every opportunity has been taken away from them or because other people have monopolized the wealth and put a fence around it.

You may be shut off from engaging in business in certain industries, or choose to not do business in certain arenas, but there are other channels open to you.

It is quite true that if you are an office worker working for a giant corporation that you have very little chance of becoming the owner of the organization in which you work; but it is also true that if you will start to act in a certain way, you can soon leave your employer and start your own business endeavors.

There is great opportunity at this time for those who will cultivate their desired skills; such people will certainly get rich. You may say that it is impossible for you to do so, but when you act upon your vision and remain consistent, you will see the success you pursue. At different periods of human history, the tide of opportunity flows in different directions according to the needs of the whole and the particular stage of social evolution which has been reached.

Today, opportunity is open before you. It is open before the person who learns to tap into their creativity and act upon it. There is abundance of opportunity for the person who will work with or despite the tide, instead of trying to swim against it. Employees, either as individuals or as "the working class," are not often directly deprived of opportunity in most places.

The workers in most of the world are not being "kept down" by their masters as they may be in more brutal places. Most people are not being forced to stay down or remain employed by giant corporations or business conglomerates in conditions they despise. As a class, employees are where they are because they do not do things in a certain way. If the working class chose to do so, they could follow the example of many others throughout history who have built their own successful organizations through perseverance, trial and error, and cooperating with others who have similar vision and values - and they don't have to do so with greed or malice. They could elect people of their own class to office, and pass laws favoring the development of more cooperative industries. In a few years they could take peaceable possession of the business and industrial fields by setting new and better examples of what is possible.

The working & creative class will become the dominant class whenever they begin and continue to do things in a certain way. The law of wealth is the same for them as it is for all others.

The average worker will remain exactly where they are until they begin thinking and acting differently. The individual worker *(that's you)*, however, is not held down by the ignorance or the mindsets of his co-workers. You can create a tide of opportunity to riches. No one is kept in poverty by a shortness in the supply of riches. There is more than enough for all. Homes could be built for every family on earth from the building material in the United States alone if conditions were right and new systems and technologies were established to do so. With the right intentions and conditions, we can produce enough fabric and food to clothe and feed everyone quite well. We must abandon the greed that prevents this reality.

The visible supply is practically inexhaustible, and the invisible supply really IS inexhaustible. Everything you see on earth is made from one original formless substance and energy, out of which all things proceed. New forms are constantly being made, and older ones are dissolving, but all things that exist are made up of the same basic building blocks of life. There is no limit to the supply of formless stuff or original substance. The universe is made out of it, and it was not all used up in making the universe. The spaces in, through, and between the forms of the visible universe are permeated and filled with that original substance / energy and the raw creative material of all things. You can work with that creative material to make new things. Once those things are made, you can assign value to them.

54

Ten thousand times more things than those that already exist might still be made, and even then we would not have exhausted the supply of universal raw material. No person, therefore, is poor because nature is poor or because there is not enough to go around.

Nature is an inexhaustible storehouse of riches. The supply will never run short if the earth is cultivated properly. The original substance is alive with creative energy, and is constantly producing more forms. When the supply of building material is exhausted, more can be produced. When the soil is exhausted so that food stuffs and materials for clothing will no longer grow upon it, the ground can rest and be renewed and more soil can be made. Architecture, humanity, and systems can be designed and developed to work *with* nature instead of just working to profit from it. When all the wood, stone, gold and silver has been dug from the earth, if humanity is still in such a stage of social development that we need wood, stone, gold and silver, more will produced from the formless or new technologies will be invented to replace them. The formless stuff responds to the needs of humanity; it will not let them be without any good thing. This is true of humanity collectively. Humanity as a whole is abundantly rich, and if individuals remain poor for their whole lives, it is because they do not follow the certain way of doing things which can make the individual person rich. Those in poverty can create new things and build their way towards riches through the creative method.

The formless substance is intelligent. It is substance which thinks. It is alive, and is always impelled toward more life. It is the natural and inherent impulse of life to seek to live more. It is the nature of intelligence to enlarge itself and of consciousness to seek to extend its boundaries and find fuller expression. The universe of forms has been made by a formless living substance, throwing itself into various forms in order to express itself more fully. The universe is a great living presence, always moving inherently toward more life and fuller functioning. Nature is formed for the advancement of life. Its impelling motive is the increase of life. For this cause, everything which can possibly minister to life is bountifully provided. You are not kept poor by lack in the supply of riches. Even the resources of the formless supply are at the command of the man or woman who will act and think in a certain way. You must stop thinking about your state of poverty and meditate on what you can create to get out of poverty. You do not need to compete.

Some thoughts on this chapter...

It is definitely a bit of a mental hurdle to process what Wattles is saying in this chapter. At least it was for me. It requires you to consider the fact that if you are in the employ of an organization that treats you poorly, you are, in fact, likely free to quit and set out on your own. He is not implying that it is an easy road - simply that few are forced to remain in an employment situation with which they are genuinely unhappy (except in obviously extreme circumstances). I do not believe the author is attempting to tell you what specific type of industry you should consider going into. I believe he is suggesting that you not stress out so much over trying to build something in a heavily competitive arena and instead focus your attention more on areas of interest to you and things that would not involve unnecessary competition. Two excellent books on this topic are "Purple Cow" by Seth Godin and "Blue Ocean Strategy" by W. Chan Kim and Renée Mauborgne.

You will notice throughout this book that Wattles suggests repeatedly to stay mentally on the creative plane, not the competitive one. *More on this later. Just a heads up, this is around the area of the book where some folks might scoff at the concepts and things may get a bit too "woo-woo" for your tastes. I would encourage you to keep reading despite any of those frustrations, as I dealt with them myself when I first read it. If it doesn't resonate with you, no worries. Just skip those parts and keep going.*

Don't get stuck on semantics here.

Thinking about this like you are simply working with your imagination has been one way to ponder these ideas that has been less woo and more practical for me. When he speaks of "original substance" and "formless substance," if that feels too weird for you, try just replacing it with words like matter, universal energy, atoms, the cosmos, or something along those lines in the scientific sense. No need to overanalyze the philosophies here.

Nobody knows exactly how we all got here. *The sooner you can admit that to yourself, the sooner you can focus on the infinite number of things you CAN prove, fix, enjoy, create, design, build, and do instead of lost in endless, foolish, and fruitless politicized debates about spirituality vs. science.*

What if it's both? Who cares? C'mon, people. *If you want to look at it from a spiritual standpoint, cool. You can look at tapping into your creative power as a way of connecting with and honoring God as Creator. Do not mistake the concepts discussed here and going forward as an excuse to set aside the responsibility we have a species to properly steward our natural resources on this planet, however. As much as it depends on us, I believe we should do so in an environmentally responsible way. I am all for creating sustainable clean energy and production solutions, and doing all that we can to solve the myriad of crises that previous generations of greed and disregard for the planet have created. The fact that this is even a debate is completely bonkers to me. Why would you want to live on a polluted planet?*

Either way, if you are in a particularly bad financial situation or were born into abject poverty, do not read any of this as an attack on you *or as if we are minimizing how difficult your life currently is or has been. We are simply saying that regardless of location or circumstance, there are certain principles that, if followed, will eventually lead you to a better quality of life. In simple terms, making money and growing your base of wealth is all about tapping into your own inherent creative power and bringing things of value into this world that others will buy and/or pay you for. This is ALL work - but you're already working anyway, so why not work towards creating something of unique value that you believe in?*

Remember - always do what you can with what you have where you are. We will keep coming back to this point.

Never mistake motion for action.

- Ernest Hemingway -

chapter 4:
the first principle

Thought is the only power which can produce tangible riches from formless substance. Applying your imagination and creativity to some type of formless substance can lead to producing what you have imagined.

All substances and creations begin first with thought. Every form and process and object that you see in nature is the visible expression of a thought that has been applied to some original and formless substance. As thought and imagination is applied to a formless substance, it takes that form. That is the way all things were created. We live in a thought world, which is part of a thought universe. Every thought of a form held in thinking substance causes the creation of the form, usually along the lines of growth and action already established.

If you had the thought of a particular style of house and impressed that thought upon a formless substance, it might not cause the instant formation of the house... but it would cause the turning of creative energies already working in trade and commerce into such channels, which would eventually result in the building of the house.

Humanity is a thinking center and can originate thought. All the things that humanity fashions with their hands must first exist in their minds. One cannot shape a thing until one has thought of that thing.

So far humanity has confined their efforts wholly to the work of their hands; they have applied manual labor to the world of forms, seeking to change or modify those already existing. Many have never thought of trying to cause the creation of new forms by impressing their thoughts upon formless substances.

When you have an idea, you take material from the forms of nature and make an image of the idea (or form) which is in your mind. You have, so far, made little or no effort to cooperate with the formless intelligence. Humanity reshapes and modifies existing forms by manual labor. Few have given much attention to the question whether they may not produce things from formless substance by communicating their thoughts to it. I propose to prove that you may do this, to prove that any man or woman may do this, and to show you how. As our first step, we must lay down some fundamental propositions.

First, we assert that there is one original formless stuff, or substance, from which all things are made.

All of the seemingly many elements are but different presentations of one element. The various forms found in organic and inorganic nature are but different shapes, made from the same basic stuff / raw materials - and this stuff is thinking stuff. Applying your imagination and creativity to these formless substances can produce the form of the original thoughts. **Applying your thoughts to formless substances produces shapes.** Humanity is a thinking center, capable of original thought. If humanity can communicate their thoughts to the original thinking substance, they can cause the creation, or formation, of the things they think about. Humanity has the power to cause the formation of the things they think about and imagine.

To summarize this:

- There is a thinking stuff from which all things are made, and which, in its original state, permeates, penetrates, and fills the empty spaces of the universe.

- A thought in this substance produces the thing that is imagined by the thought.

- Humanity can form things in their thoughts, and by impressing their thoughts upon formless substance can cause the things they think about to be created.

Sound weird? Don't worry...

*As mentioned earlier, if this seems weird or confusing, replace the phrase "formless stuff / substance" with matter, atoms, or energy in the scientific sense. What he means entirely by "this stuff is thinking stuff" is something I still ponder on but don't pay too much attention to, so try not to get stuck there. I would also add that just sitting around and thinking about things that you want to create isn't going to get you very far. Thinking about the things that you want to create and then actually taking practical action to make them happen is how this works. It's not rocket science. It's work. A lot of people can get tripped up on this kind of book because they perceive that those who advocate reading them are insinuating that it's just some "name it and claim it" concept or "new age thinking." Without adding the element of **taking practical, present action, you're not going to reach your goals. It really is that simple...but nobody said it was easy.***

Sitting in a room at some Himalayan retreat center and thinking about writing a book is not going to magically produce the book that you want to write. You have to actually sit down and write the book!

*It's great to first have those initial and original thoughts - however, it is what you **do** with those thoughts that will determine what happens next.*

A person's way of doing things is the direct result of the way they think about things.

I have said that humanity gets rich by doing things in a certain way and in order to do so, humanity must learn to think in a certain way. To do things in the way you want to do them, you will have to acquire the ability to think the way you want to think. This is the first step toward getting rich.

To think what you want to think is to channel your mind and focus on your goals regardless of current appearances and circumstances.

Every person has the natural and inherent power to think what they want to think, but it requires far more effort to do so than it does to think the thoughts which are suggested by appearances. To think according to appearance is easy; to think and focus on your goals and truth regardless of appearances is laborious and often requires the expenditure of more power than any other work humanity is called upon to perform. There is no labor from which most people shrink as they do from that of sustained and consecutive thought. It is the hardest work in the world. This is especially true when truth is contrary to appearances. Every appearance in the visible world tends to produce a corresponding form in the mind which observes it, and this can only be prevented by holding the thought of the truth.

To meditate upon the appearances of disease will produce the form / image of disease and fear in your own mind and ultimately in your body. There are always things you can do to work on improving your health: physically, emotionally, and mentally. Put simply, complaining about and focusing on negative health circumstances will not help you. Focus on what you can do to improve.

To meditate upon the appearances of poverty will produce corresponding forms / images and fear in your own mind and ultimately in your bank account or life. There are always things you can do to work on improving your financial health and education. Put simply, complaining about or focusing on how poor you are will not help you. Focus on what you can create to get out of poverty.

It takes power and diligence to think and meditate about health when surrounded by the appearances of disease or to think and meditate about building or growing riches when in the midst of circumstances of poverty. However, those who acquire and cultivate this power become MASTER MINDS. They can conquer fate and have what they want. This power can only be acquired by getting hold of the basic fact which is behind all appearances: that fact is that there is one thinking substance from which and by which all things are made.

We must grasp the truth that every thought or idea held in this substance can become a thing. Humanity can impress their thoughts upon formless substances, bring form to them, and turn what once was formless into tangible, usable, visible, and valuable things.

We can create what we want to create, we can make what we want to have, and we can become who we want to be. Once you realize this, you can train yourself to lose all doubt and fear. You can train yourself to focus on creating, not competing. As a first step toward getting rich, you must believe the three fundamental statements given previously in this chapter, and in order to emphasize them, I repeat them here:

- There is a thinking stuff from which all things are made, and which, in its original state, permeates, penetrates, and fills the empty spaces of the universe.

- A thought in this substance produces the thing that is imagined by the thought.

- Humanity can form things in their thoughts, and by impressing their thoughts upon formless substance can cause the things they think about to be created.

You must dwell upon this until it is fixed in your mind and has become your habitual, subconscious thought. Read these creed statements over and over again. Fix every word upon your memory and meditate upon them until you firmly grasp what they say. If a doubt comes to you, cast it aside. Do not listen to arguments against this idea. Do not go to churches or lectures where a contrary concept of things is taught or preached. Do not read magazines, newspapers, or books which teach a different idea. If you get mixed up in your faith, all your efforts will be in vain.

Okay, that may have gotten a little "woo"...

This chapter can be easy to get stuck on - especially if all you do is look around at the state of the world today. There is plenty of disease, poverty, lack, racism, fear, war, and things of that sort that would certainly seem to contradict Wattles' statements by this point in the book. There are lots of examples of current physical realities that are the polar opposite of what many of us want to be true. All we can change is where we choose to place our focus and what we do next. That's what this book is about and what we will keep coming back to. Keep focused on what you can control.

Wishing things had been different or better in the past gets you nowhere.

Instead of getting stuck on these spots in the book, try to look at it like this: we've all had those scenarios where we feel a random pain somewhere in our body and then go looking around the internet to try and figure out what it might be. We end up on a myriad of different websites and in no time we are convinced that we have stage 27 cancer, diabetes, and some rare disease that we didn't even know existed until ten minutes ago, all because we spent just a short amount of time "meditating upon the appearance of disease." The statistical odds of **actually** having those diseases is - at least in most cases - very, very small - but the likelihood of instilling vast amounts of fear in our minds after looking at all of that stuff is very, very high. Fear and stress can lead to all kinds of diseases, which is why it's not advisable to waste your time or mental energy looking at those kinds of things on the internet and worrying about it further.

If you are genuinely concerned about your health, go and see a licensed and trusted medical doctor. Don't go browsing around the web looking for self-diagnoses. Don't think that memes you see shared on social media or sketchy internet videos with creepy music qualify as actual medical advice. I would say the same about financial struggles and poverty. If you are in a dire financial situation, spending all your time and energy fretting or complaining about it does you no good. It is a total waste of your focus and creativity. Instead, **choose** - (yes, it's a choice) - to read, watch, learn, and do all you can to better your financial situation.

Learn from those who have attained the kind of financial success that you seek. Use your creative energies to invest in your potential and learn everything you can about how to better tap into the vast sources of abundance that this world has to offer. You can choose to do this instead of stressing yourself out worrying about your current financial state or the financial state of others. Choose to convert that energy into positive, creative action. It takes practice – a lot of it – but the payoff is worth it.

~~~~~~~~~~~~~~~~

To elaborate a bit further on the concepts in this chapter, especially if it still feels a little too 'woo-woo' for you, look at it like this: you need to first imagine/form the thought in your mind of a blue duck before you can paint a blue duck on an empty (formless) canvas (substance).

***Another example:** you need to first think about the shape you want to create in a piece of pottery before you can actually begin to bring form to that piece of clay. See? Formless substance really can boil down to just about any kind of blank document, an empty canvas or room, a blank piece of paper, or a lump of clay. Once you apply your own imagination to work upon that formless substance, the creative magic starts to happen. It is impossible that Mr. Wattles would have thought about the technological advances of things like 3D printing in his day, and that is just one more example of these concepts in action. We truly do live in an era where you can dream up and design something from nothing. There is technology available today that can make the creation of your ideas happen astronomically faster than when this book was originally published. There are already places that are 3D printing houses in a single day! The biggest encouragement I can give you is to learn as much as you can about harnessing the creative process and bringing your own ideas to life. It will serve you well in the future AND it's so much fun.*

Additionally, as I've said elsewhere, I would not advise blind allegiance to any creed or concept as Wattles suggests at the end of this chapter. *Test everything out for yourself as a scientist would. I have found that a lot of the concepts in this book have been helpful in my journey, but I would not turn it into a religion/dogma and insist that people just fall in line and believe me just because I say so. No thanks! Not my shtick.*

Try things out and then keep doing what works for you and brings you joy, not dread. Drudgery is not sustainable.

~~~~~~~~~~~~~~~~

Try not to get caught up in the dogma or super-spiritual sounding nature of different portions of the book and look at it like you are working with your imagination and the creative power we all inherently have within us. There are great mysteries about how we got here and spiritual beliefs that have been hotly debated for thousands of years – and I have wasted far too much time engaging in those kinds of debates. I'm not interested in that. What I'm interested in is how we can tap into our own creativity here and now and use it to make the world a better place than we found it.

The best thing you can do for others in a state of poverty is to teach them how to get out of it. If you are in poverty yourself, the best thing you can do is to learn how to get out of it...not to sit and complain about how broke you are. It **will** take time and dedicated effort - often more time than any of us would like - but there are countless books, courses, mentors, stories, biographies, and videos that you can help you learn how to get out of bad financial situations. What do you have to lose by trying?

You can learn new skills that will help you find new opportunities. There are often community resources that may be of help to you. Ask around and use the internet to find the assistance you need. There is no shame in asking for help. Don't let the noise in your head or cultural propaganda that says otherwise stop you from getting help if you truly need it. The people who insist on everyone "pulling themselves up by their bootstraps" without a shred of empathy or compassion for others are not the kinds of people whose opinions you should be paying attention to.

Again: I deeply understand how it feels to not know where your next rent check is coming from, how you're going to pay those medical, student loan, or credit card bills, or how you're going to keep food on the table for your family. I know what it's like to need to depend on gifts and the kindness of others when money is tight. It is not fun, but it is also not permanent if you **choose to devote yourself to getting out of that hole** and put in the work required to do so. You've got this. Keep going.

Action will remove
the doubts that theory
cannot solve.

- Tehyi Hsieh -

chapter 5:
increasing life

You must get rid of the last hint of the old idea that there is a deity whose will it is that you should be poor or whose purposes may be served by keeping you in poverty.

The intelligent substance which is in all things and lives in everything also lives in you. It is a consciously living substance. Being a consciously living substance, it must have the nature and inherent desire of every living intelligence for the increase of life. Every living thing must continually seek for the enlargement of its life because life - in the mere act of living - must increase itself.

When a seed is dropped into the ground, it springs into activity. In the act of living, it produces hundreds or thousands more seeds. Life, by living and by definition, multiplies itself. It is forever becoming more; it must do so, if it continues to be at all. Intelligence is under this same necessity for continuous increase. Every thought we think makes it necessary for us to think another thought. Our consciousness is continually expanding. Every fact we learn leads us to the learning of another fact. Knowledge is continually increasing.

Every talent that we cultivate brings to the mind the desire to cultivate another talent. We are subject to the urge of life. While seeking the expression of that urge, we are driven to know more, to do more, and to be more.

In order to know more, do more, and be more we must have more. We must have things to use. Why? Because we learn, and do, and become, only by using things.

Therefore, we must get rich so that we can live more.

The desire for riches is simply the capacity for larger life seeking fulfillment. Every desire is the effort of an unexpressed possibility to become a reality.

It is power seeking to manifest itself which causes desire. That which makes you want more money is the same as that which makes the plant grow. It is life, and it is seeking fuller expression. The one living substance must be subject to this inherent law of all life. It is permeated with the desire to live more and that is why it is under the necessity of creating things. Since this desire to live and express more is also within you, it wants you to have all the things you can use.

More does not always = happy. Enough = happy.

The fact that you are even reading this book is proof of the desire to expand your life. You would not be reading a book called 'The Science of Getting Rich' if you did not have some inherent desire for more wealth, more freedom to express yourself, and more freedom to do the things that wealth provides. However, do not mistakenly think that simply having more money will make you happier. While making sure that your basic needs are met is oftentimes a source of great unrest and it is a huge relief when those dire financial problems are no more, lasting happiness is not something that occurs just because you have more money in the bank.

Happiness is an internal state and most times is the result of choices that we make, the perspectives we adopt and stories we believe about our circumstances, the actions we take, and the kinds of people we surround ourselves with. There are plenty of stories of exceedingly wealthy people who are miserable, depressed, alone or who have broken families because of their own issues with greed, deception, and things of that sort. Make sure to get your priorities straight on this path. You don't want the miserable life of those who pursue money just for selfish gain or greed. Read the excellent book "The Soul of Money" by Lynne Twist to explore this concept further.

It is the desire of God that you should get rich. God wants you to get rich because he can express himself better through you if you have plenty of things to use in giving him expression. God can live more in you if you have unlimited command of the means of life. The universe desires you to have everything you want to have. Nature is friendly to your plans. Everything is naturally for you. Make up your mind that this is true.

It is essential, however that your purpose should harmonize with the purpose that is in all things. You must want real life, not mere pleasure or sensual gratification. Life is the performance of function, and the individual really lives only when they perform every function (physical, mental, and spiritual) of which they are capable, without excess in any.

You do not want to get rich in order to live swinishly for the gratification of animal desires. That is not life. However, the performance of every physical function is a part of life, and no one lives completely who denies the impulses of the body a normal and healthy expression. You do not want to get rich solely to enjoy mental pleasures, to get knowledge, to gratify ambition, to outshine others, or to be famous. All of these are a legitimate part of life, but the person who lives for the pleasures of the intellect alone will only have a partial life, and they will never be satisfied with their lot.

You do not want to get rich solely for the good of others, to lose yourself for the salvation of mankind, to experience the joys of philanthropy and sacrifice. The joys of the soul are only a part of life, and they are no better or nobler than any other part.

You want to get rich in order that you may eat, drink, and be merry when it is time to do these things. You want to get rich in order that you may surround yourself with beautiful things, see distant lands, feed your mind, and develop your intellect.

You want to be rich so that you may love those around you and those you care about, do kind things, and be able to play a good part in helping the world to find truth.

Just remember that extreme altruism is no better and no nobler than extreme selfishness – both are mistakes.

Get rid of the idea that God wants you to sacrifice yourself for others, and that you can secure special favors by doing so. God requires nothing of the kind.

What God wants is that you should make the most of yourself, for yourself, and for others. You can help others by making the most of yourself more than in any other way. You can make the most of yourself only by getting rich, so it is right and praiseworthy that you should give your first and best thought to the work of acquiring wealth.

Remember, however, that the desire of the universe is for all, and its movements must be for more life to all. It cannot be made to work for less life to any, because it is equally in all, seeking riches and life.

The intelligent substance will make things for you, but it will not take things away from someone else in order to give them to you.

There's more than enough to go around.

Keep in mind here that the author is not suggesting that the end-all, be-all is financial gain or that the only way you can make something of yourself is by making more money. That is not the point...at least not as I understand it.

Without having our basic financial needs met and having enough material wealth in order to do the things that we have in our hearts to do, we end up striving, anxious, depressed, and struggling in our creative pursuits.

When that is the case, often people end up getting stuck in the competitive, not the creative mind. As we will explore shortly, that's a trap.

It is only once we overcome our fear of not having enough or being enough that we truly are able to lean into our creative power and operate from a place of power and authentic expression.

You must get rid of the thought of competition. You are to create, not to compete for what is already created.

You do not have to take anything away from anyone. You do not have to drive sharp bargains. You do not have to cheat, or to take advantage. You do not need to let anyone work for you for less than they earn or for less than a wage that they can actually live on. You do not have to covet the property of others, or to look at it with wishful eyes.

No one has anything of which you cannot have the like, and you can do so without taking what they have away from them or harming anyone else in the process.

You are to become a creator, not a competitor.

No other creature on earth has been granted the creative abilities that you have, and when you learn to harness that creative power, you tap into something beyond yourself.

You are going to get what you want, but you will get it in such a way that when you get it, every other person will have more than they have now. I am aware that there are those who get a vast amount of money by acting in direct opposition to the statements in the paragraph above, and want to add a word of explanation here.

There are those of the plutocratic and competitive type who become very rich sometimes purely by their extraordinary ability to act on the plane of competition. Sometimes they unconsciously align themselves with the infinite substance in its great purposes and movements through their contributions to the evolution of various industries.

Rockefeller, Andrew Carnegie, JP Morgan, and those of their type have been the unconscious agents of the supreme powers that are in the necessary work of systematizing and organizing productive industry. In the end, their work will contribute immensely toward increased life for all, but their day is nearly over. They have organized production, and will soon be succeeded by the agents of the multitude, who will organize the machinery and lead systems of distribution.

The ultra-mega wealthy are like the monster reptiles of the prehistoric eras. They play a necessary part in the evolutionary process, but the same power which produced them will eventually be rid of them.

It is well to bear in mind that the ultra-rich have never been really rich in the fullest sense of the word. A record of the private lives of most of this class will show that they have really been the most abject and wretched of the poor.

Riches secured on the competitive plane are never satisfactory and permanent. They are yours today and another's tomorrow. Remember: if you are to become rich in a scientific and certain way, you must rise entirely out of the competitive mindset and focus on the creative one. You must never think for a moment that the supply is limited.

Just as soon as you begin to think that all the money is being "cornered" and controlled by bankers and others and that you must stress yourself out to get laws passed to stop this process and so on - it is in that moment that you drop into the competitive mind. This is where your power to cause creation is gone for the time being, and what is worse, you will probably slow down or stop the creative movements you have already begun.

...okay, Wattles - but look around! Everything is pretty screwed up!

I am the first to admit that if I spend even a few minutes looking at "the news" or mindlessly browsing social media and the infinite number of articles or videos that are published every day, I can burn out and get overwhelmed very quickly. The for-profit news media spends so much time, energy, and money heralding all of the various types of corruption, power-grabs, and politicking that goes on in the competitive financial and political arenas.

It probably leaves you feeling helpless, afraid, and powerless to do anything positive in this world because, well hey - look at how terrible things can be! There is so much fear, uncertainty and finger-pointing that it renders the creative spark almost completely useless - at least until I'm able to snap out of it and get back to building and creating. That is what I believe Wattles is addressing in this chapter. It's not that you shouldn't care about the goings-on in your community or stick your head in the sand. It is that your energy and focus is best spent CREATING and relentlessly paying more attention to the things that are within your control – not consuming all of the drama and noise of the world that you can't control which just results in fear, rage, anxiety, depression, and inaction. Even in Wattles' day – as all throughout human history to date – there was the class of people that today many would call "the 1%."

*These types are those who seem to have an unbelievable amount of material wealth, control, and power. Rockefeller, Carnegie, JP Morgan, and others wielded immense influence over the way things developed in the United States especially, and undoubtedly there were a lot of not-so-nice things that they did to maintain that power. Today, you could say the same of some of the mega-billionaires and corporate robber barons of our day. But really think about this for a moment: **is that the kind of wealth that you are genuinely after by reading a book like this?** If it is, you're reading the wrong book. I do not view that kind of exorbitant material wealth, power, and control as a lifestyle to aspire to.*

I view it as the kind of life to pity and turn away from. *Do you think that it's easy to trust anyone when you make millions of dollars a day? Do you think that they are carefree, happy people? Do you think their family lives are healthy and that they have a lot of close friends (that aren't on their payroll)? Likely not. I wouldn't encourage aspiring towards trying to become some monopolist or mega-billionaire. Those who do aim in this direction are likely pursuing power for the sake of power...and a simple glance through the history books shows how well that usually plays out. Cultivate gratitude as you grow and keep creating. That way is better.*

Focus on your sphere of influence and what you can control.

I would be willing to bet that you'd much rather focus on finding creative ways to ensure that your needs and the needs of your loved ones are met than you would trying to become the latest version of a celebrity or corporate overlord. I'd also be willing to bet that you'd like to genuinely enjoy the riches and blessings that you have with as little drama as possible. (That is, without the opportunity cost and craziness that comes with having to take an army of lawyers, bodyguards, and emotional baggage everywhere you go. No thanks.)

What Wattles is saying here is sound advice: essentially, don't stress yourself out so much about those who seem to have limitless supplies of financial wealth and power...and don't waste your energy trying to become like them. Focus on what you can do to bring value into the world. Focus on what you can create and build your own creative endeavors. Develop your art. Write that book or that screenplay. Apply for that better job. Work on that side hustle until you can leave your 9-5. You do not need to compete in order to do this.

Lastly, just a reminder if all of this still feels too overtly spiritual - when thinking of "formless substance," remind yourself that everything around you that you can see was first without form. Every object that is around you right at this very moment at one time only existed in someone else's mind. You too can harness that creative power and generate true wealth for yourself and those you care about.

KNOW that there are countless millions of dollars' worth of gold in the mountains of the earth, not yet brought to light. Know that if there were not, more would be created from the thinking substance to supply your needs.

KNOW that the money you need will come, even if it is necessary for a thousand people to be led to the discovery of new gold mines tomorrow.

Never look at the visible supply - look always at the limitless riches in the formless substance, and KNOW that they are coming to you as fast as you can receive and use them. Nobody, by cornering the visible supply, can prevent you from getting what is yours. Never allow yourself to think for an instant that all the best building spots will be taken before you get ready to build your house unless you hurry.

Never worry about the trusts and giant corporations and get anxious and fear that they will soon come to own the whole earth. Doing so is not useful. Never be afraid that you will lose what you want because some other person "beats you to it."

That cannot possibly happen, for you are not seeking anything that is possessed by anybody else. You are causing what you want to be created from the formless substance, and the supply of creativity within you is without limits.

Stick to the basics:

- There is a thinking stuff from which all things are made, and which, in its original state, permeates, penetrates, and fills the empty spaces of the universe.

- A thought in this substance produces the thing that is imagined by the thought.

- Humanity can form things in their thoughts, and by impressing their thoughts upon formless substance can cause the things they think about to be created.

We are what we
repeatedly do.

Excellence, then,
is not an act,
but a habit.

- Will Durant -

chapter 6:
how riches come to you

You do not have to get something for nothing, but you can give to every person more than you take from them.

When I say that you do not have to drive sharp bargains, I do not mean that you do not have to drive any bargains at all, or that you are above the necessity for having any dealings with your fellow person. I mean that you will not need to deal with them unfairly. You cannot give every person more in cash market value than you take from them, but you can give them more in use value than the cash value of the thing you take from them. The paper, ink, and other material in this book may not be worth the money you pay for it, but if the ideas suggested by it bring you thousands of dollars, you have not been wronged by those who sold it to you - **they have given you a great use value for a small cash value.**

Let us suppose that I own a picture by one of the great artists, which, in any civilized community, is worth a large amount of money. Say then that I take it to a very cold area in the Arctic, and by "salesmanship" encourage one of the inhabitants of this area to give me a bundle of furs worth $500 for the painting. I have really wronged him, for he has no use for the picture. **It has no use value to him and thus it will not add to his quality of life.**

But suppose I give him supplies and resources to help him live better in his climate for his furs. In this way, we have made a good bargain. He has use for the supplies - they will help him and will add more benefits to his life. They will make him richer than he was before our deal. When you rise from the competitive to the creative plane, you can scan your business transactions very strictly, and if you are selling any person anything which does not add more to their life than the thing they give you in exchange, you can afford to stop it.

You do not have to compete or work to beat anybody in business. If you are in a business which makes you compete with people, get out of it at once.

Give everyone more in use value than you take from them in cash value. It is then that you are adding to the life of the world by every business transaction. If you have employees, you can so organize your business and work place culture so that it will be filled with the principle of advancement. In this way, each employee who wishes to do so may advance more in their work and development every day.

You can make your business do for your employees what this book is doing for you. You can conduct your business in a way that it will be a sort of ladder by which every employee who will works towards it may climb to riches themselves. If they are given the opportunity but do not do so, it is not your fault.

Keep in mind that just because you are to cause the creation of your riches from the formless substance which permeates all of your environment, it does not mean that they will immediately take shape from the atmosphere and come into being right before your eyes.

If you want a sewing machine, for instance, I do not mean to tell you that you are to imagine or visualize a sewing machine until it is formed out of thin air in the room where you currently are. But if you want a sewing machine, hold the mental image of it with the most positive certainty that it is being made or is on its way to you. After once forming the thought, have the most absolute and unquestioning faith that the sewing machine is coming. Never think or speak of it in any other way than being en route to you.

Claim it as already yours...because you aren't competing here. You are creating from the formless and bringing forth something unique.

It will be brought to you by the power of the supreme intelligence, acting upon the minds of humanity. If you live in Maine, it may be that someone will be brought from Texas or Japan to engage in some transaction which will result in your getting what you want. If so, the whole matter will be as much to that person's advantage as it is to yours.

"Already mine?" Is this guy nuts?!

As mentioned elsewhere, this is one of those areas of the book where people might get caught up in the whole "name it-claim it" thing. At least for me, I have tried to not get stuck on this stuff and re-frame it as just learning how to form clear, focused goals.

When you are setting definite goals for yourself, you obviously have to form a clear mental picture of those goals and keep believing that it is possible to achieve them in order for you to see them come to fruition. At least in my own experience, I have found that rarely do things come to me in the time frame that I would like them to - but if I consistently pursue the goals I set for myself, eventually I do see them achieved. (Although I have never really wanted a sewing machine as Wattles talks about at length here!)

*This is not rocket science, of course - but I believe what Wattles is getting at is to remind you, dear reader, to not lose hope. Do not give up or abandon your thoughts to doubts and fear when in the pursuit of your goals. **It is simply not useful.***

Do not forget for a moment that the thinking substance is in all things, communicating with everyone, and can influence everything. The desire of the thinking substance for fuller life and better living has caused the creation of all the sewing machines that have already been made and it can cause the creation of millions more. It will do this whenever people set these things in motion by desire, faith and by acting in a certain way.

You can certainly have a sewing machine in your house and it is just as certain that you can have any other things which you want which you will use for the advancement of your own life and the lives of others. You need not hesitate about asking for abundance. Even Jesus said, "it is your Heavenly Father's pleasure to give you the kingdom."

The original substance wants to live fully expressed in you and wants you to have all that you can or will use for the living of the most abundant life. If you fix upon your consciousness the fact that the desire you feel for the possession of riches is one with the desire of God for more complete expression of life and creativity, your faith becomes invincible.

Once I saw a little boy sitting at a piano, and vainly trying to bring harmony out of the keys. I saw that he was grieved and provoked by his inability to play real music. I asked him the cause of his frustration, and he answered, "I can feel the music in me, but I can't make my hands go right."

The music in him was the urge of the original substance, containing all the possibilities of all life. Music was seeking expression through the child. God, the one infinite substance, is trying to live and do and enjoy things through humanity. God is saying, "I want hands to build wonderful structures, to play divine harmonies, to paint glorious pictures. I want feet to run my errands, eyes to see my beauties, tongues to tell mighty truths and to sing marvelous songs," and so on.

Every possibility is seeking expression through humankind. God wants those who can play music to have pianos and every other instrument and to have the means to cultivate their talents to the fullest extent. He wants those who can appreciate beauty to be able to surround themselves with beautiful things. He wants those who can discern truth to have every opportunity to travel and observe. He wants those who can appreciate fashion to be beautifully clothed, and those who can appreciate good food to be luxuriously fed. He wants all these things because he enjoys and appreciates them. It is God who wants to play, sing, enjoy beauty, proclaim truth and wear fine clothes, and eat good foods. "It is God that works in you to will and to do," said Paul.

The desire you feel for riches is the infinite seeking to express itself in you as it sought to find expression in the little boy at the piano, so you need not hesitate to ask largely. Your part is to focus and express the desire to God.

This is a difficult point with most people. They retain something of the old idea that poverty and self-sacrifice are pleasing to God. They look upon poverty as a part of the plan for their lives – whether because of fate or because they believe God has subjected them to poverty to teach them some kind of karmic lesson through pain and suffering.

This is not a useful mentality to hold onto. They have the idea that God has finished his work and made all that he can make, and that the majority of humanity must stay poor because there is not enough to go around. They hold to so much of this erroneous thought that they feel ashamed to ask for wealth. They try not to want more than a very modest competence... just enough to make them fairly comfortable.

I recall now the case of one student who was told that he must get in mind a clear picture of the things he desired so that the creative thought of them might be impressed on the formless substance. He was a very poor man, living in a rented house, and having only what he earned from day to day. He could not grasp the fact that all wealth was his.

After thinking the matter over, he decided that he might reasonably ask for a new rug for the floor of his best room and a stove to heat the house during the cold weather.

Following the instructions given in this book, he obtained these things in a few months and then it dawned upon him that he had not asked enough. He went through the house in which he lived, and planned all the improvements he would like to make in it. He mentally added a bay window here and a room there until it was so complete in his mind as his ideal home that he even envisioned and planned the furnishings.

Holding the whole picture in his mind, he began living in the certain way and moving toward what he wanted. He owns the house now, and is rebuilding it after the form of his mental image. And now, with still larger faith, he is going on to get greater things.

It has been unto him according to his faith, and it is so with you and with all of us.

Time to get rid of that angry old-time religion.

Notice in the story above that the man first formed a clear picture of what he was wanting in his mind. So few of us even allow ourselves the luxury of slowing down and imagining what our lives could be like if we were not struggling with this problem or that problem. By exercising the power of your imagination and allowing yourself permission to dream big, you can get a clear image of what you're wanting your life to look like. I'll say that again: you have to give yourself permission to dream big. Write those dreams down. Keep them somewhere that you can see them often, like in a journal you revisit daily or on a whiteboard in your room or office. Set up and decorate your immediate environment to look like the kind of space you want to be in. This is important.

At least for me, so much of this creative journey is about reminding myself about where I want to be heading and forming clearer mental pictures of the life I want to build while focusing on my very limited sphere of control: my thoughts and my actions. Exercising my imagination and channeling my attention in this method is the only way I know how to snap out of a funk... and sometimes the best way to do that is to focus on building something better right where you are here and now. This is a choice you make, not a feeling that just shows up at random or some bolt of Divine Lightning from the heavens.

*Furthermore, regardless of what you currently believe about faith, religious beliefs, or lack thereof – just consider for a moment how so many of us were brought up. It's difficult to find a single person who **didn't** grow up in some kind of religious environment where there are doctrines taught every week that poverty, suffering, and financial hardship somehow reflect a holy or upright lifestyle. Many times these types of messages are preached by multi-millionaire religious leaders who likely paid less in taxes over the last ten years than you did on your last paycheck.*

Those who believe that type of teaching genuinely desire to be free of their poverty – but their subconscious view of God as a cruel, angry, and miserly taskmaster often prevents them from taking actions that would actually free them from their poverty or questioning their unhelpful beliefs. This includes learning and cultivating fresh skills, discovering new and more helpful perspectives, or educating themselves about cultures that are outside of their current world view or experience. Fear-based and angry teachings can create in the mind a false view about how the world really is and what is available to us in this life, here and now. As author Tim Ferriss has said, "Reality is largely negotiable."

The angry, fear-based religious teachings that many of us inherited from our upbringings or absorbed from our culture steals so much joy and creativity from our lives. (I would add that for many of us, politics and our collective addiction to outrage-inducing news and social media is a sort of religion all its own – but that's a whole different topic for a different time.) Fearful and limited beliefs prevent us from exploring new ways of bringing our ideas to life and distract us from building a better world right where we are. The negative outlook on life and the crippling shame and depression that often results from these beliefs over time can devastate or stagnate our relationships with those we care about, traumatize our mental and physical health, and severely impact our financial and emotional literacy and well-being.

Anyone who has struggled with financial difficulties can tell you that such an experience is not something that often leads to having a positive world view or treating people well. If you are struggling with poverty, you also most likely struggle in the areas of health - physically, mentally, and emotionally – or vice versa. These challenges often compound over time and feed off of one another, creating a vicious cycle of shame, guilt, anger, depression, impostor syndrome, self-sabotage, and defeatism. Most people will find it quite difficult to appreciate much of anything if their most basic needs are not met or if they are worrying about how they are going to pay the bills and put food on the table tomorrow.

*I can say all of this with confidence because **that was me**. Some days, that's **still** me. I've had plenty of sleepless nights where I didn't know where the next paycheck was coming from or how I was going to take care of my family. I've spent hours just staring into the dark, pleading with whatever God of whatever universe would care enough about me and my problems to swoop in and help me figure out whatever current financial mess I was in. Yet in the back of my head, there was still that nagging voice that would whisper at me that this was all part of God's plan for my life, or that the financial challenges I was going through was because God was mad at me for this thing or that thing.*

***What proof did I have of any of this? None whatsoever!** But I had picked those beliefs up somewhere. It wasn't until I read this book for the first time in 2014 that I really started questioning my own beliefs around money and how to get out of the hole I was in. Poverty is miserable and I would not wish it on anyone for any reason. How to define poverty is going to be different for everyone - and I am very fortunate to have never been in a situation where I was actually on the streets without a home for more than even just a few hours. I do not claim to know what extreme, abject poverty is like for one moment...but I do know what it is like to have to depend on the generosity of strangers and loved ones alike just to make it through the day and what it is like when your bank account regularly is in danger of dipping below zero with even simple grocery purchases.*

It sucks, full stop. Poverty is expensive and brutal.

Poverty is even more brutal and unforgiving when you're convinced that God is the one who gave it to you. Ditch that BS, ASAP.

No thanks. That is not a useful belief system. Especially when you find yourself praying for relief from the very God that supposedly put you into poverty in the first place! Do you see how backwards that is?

*It'd be like someone forcing you to eat a sandwich made of gravel and sadness and then after much weeping and gnashing of teeth, you turn right around and ask **them** to take the gravel and sadness out of **your** mouth. It doesn't make much sense to ask the person who put the gravel and sadness in your mouth in the first place to take it away, now does it? (You can also apply this line of reasoning to a whole lot of beliefs and mindsets in the angry, old-time religion world and it would probably benefit you to do so... but that's a whole different topic for a whole different time.)*

Gravel-and-sadness sandwiches aside, I have spent the better part of the past decade analyzing and de-constructing many of my old, angry, fear-based beliefs and had to reckon with how completely unhelpful – and even how destructive – they were. I had to unlearn many harmful and hurtful mindsets that I had picked up in certain religious or cultural settings over the years. It's only now after years of therapy, grace, love, patience, and forgiveness from those around me that I have been able to get to a point where I can look back and see genuine progress in these areas and that I've cultivated more helpful beliefs. Nobody ever said this road was easy...but it is worth it.

Throughout human history, religious and political dogma and manipulation have been used to control the masses and take advantage of the poor by asking them to donate the little that they have to their organizations (who oftentimes are run by leaders that live very lavish lifestyles). While I certainly do not advocate living in excess and giving in to greed, I also do not adhere to the worldview that any higher power would want us as a species to remain in poverty. I used to believe otherwise and found out the hard way that it is not healthy and not useful to give those kinds of teachings any credence in my life. My life is much better now that I have intentionally cultivated more room for grace, peace, gratitude, and creativity in my world instead of listening to the voices of fear, anger, despair, and hopeless fatalism.

This is a choice, not a feeling. The right feelings come by focusing on the right things.

If you are truly struggling and feel like you are at your breaking point, let me be very clear: there is no shame in asking for and seeking help – in any capacity.

Don't buy into the propaganda and current cultural stigma that says if you need help that you're a lazy loser just looking for hand-outs. Those beliefs aren't helpful either. Sometimes life can feel like someone force-fed you a gravel-and-sadness sandwich and you won't know which way is up. The path you've traveled has brought you to this point so far. I promise you that it is a sign of great strength and courage to admit to yourself that you need help – and to choose to do what you need to in order to get and stay better. It is weakness and pride to pretend like we can do it all on our own.

*Help will look different depending on you and your situation, but it **could** look like any of the following: talking with a therapist or counselor, telling some close friends or loved ones about your struggles and that you aren't sure what to do to do next, going for a long walk and immersing yourself in nature or somewhere beautiful, contacting your local social services agencies and seeing if you and your family qualify for various types of assistance available, or joining some sort of program or class to help you snap out of whatever unhealthy patterns have emerged in your life.*

You are here for a reason.

*If no one has ever told you this, I will: I believe in you. Your voice matters and you are far more important than whatever numbers are currently showing up in your bank account or whatever job you currently have or don't have. I'll say it again, especially if your current situation feels truly dire or hopeless: **there is no shame in asking for and seeking help.** It is a sign of great courage and strength to admit to yourself and others when you are struggling. It is in that place of awareness and seeking that healing can truly begin. Don't struggle alone. You don't have to. **Ask for help.***

Success seems to be
largely a matter of
hanging on after
others have let go.

- William Feather -

chapter 7:
the power of gratitude

The whole process of cultivating a richer and more creative life can be summed up in one word: gratitude.

The illustrations given in the last chapter will have conveyed to the reader the fact that the first step towards getting rich is to focus your imagination and intention on the formless substance and to convey the idea of your desires towards it. You will see that in order to do so, it becomes necessary to relate yourself to the formless intelligence in a harmonious way. To secure this harmonious relationship is a matter of such primary and vital importance that I shall give some space to its discussion here and give you instructions which, if you will follow them, will help to bring you into perfect unity and peace with the mind of God.

First, you believe that there is one intelligent substance, from which all things proceed. Second, you believe that this substance gives you everything you desire, and third, you relate yourself to it by a feeling of deep and profound gratitude. Many people who order their lives rightly in all other ways are kept in poverty by their lack of gratitude. Having received one gift from God, they cut the wires which connect them with God's blessings by failing to cultivate gratitude. It is easy to understand that the nearer we live to the source of wealth, the more wealth we shall receive, and it is easy also to understand that the soul that is always grateful lives in closer touch with God than the one which never looks to him in thankful acknowledgment.

The more gratefully we fix our minds on the source of everything when good things come to us, the more good things we will receive, and the more rapidly they will come. The reason simply is that the mental attitude of gratitude draws the mind into closer touch with the source from which the blessings come.

If it is a new thought to you that gratitude brings your whole mind into closer harmony with the creative energies of the universe, consider it well, and you will see that it is true. The good things you already own have come to you because you have acted upon certain laws of the universe in a certain way, whether you realize it or not.

Gratitude helps position you mentally to receive the gifts and realization of the goals that you seek. It will keep you in close harmony with creative thought and prevent you from falling into competitive thought. **Remember: you are to be a creator, not a competitor.**

Gratitude alone can keep you looking toward that which is infinite and prevent you from falling into the error of thinking of the supply as limited. To do that would be fatal to your hopes.

There is a law of gratitude and it is absolutely necessary that you should observe the law if you are to get the results you seek. The law of gratitude is the natural principle that action and reaction are always equal and in opposite directions. The grateful outreaching of your mind in thankful praise to God *(or the universe, or the formless substance - however you currently define the means by which we got here)* is a an expenditure of creative force. It cannot fail to reach that to which it is addressed, and the reaction is an instantaneous movement towards you. As the old scripture says, *"Draw near to God, and he will draw near to you."*

If your gratitude is strong and constant, the reaction in the formless substance will be strong and continuous. The movement of the things you want will be always toward you. Notice the grateful attitude that even Jesus took; how he always seemed to be saying things like, *"I thank you, Father, that you hear me"* instead of taking a posture of begging and pleading in prayer. You cannot exercise much creative power without gratitude, for it is gratitude that keeps you connected with that creative power.

The value of gratitude does not consist solely in getting you more blessings in the future. Without gratitude, it won't be long before you are feeling dissatisfied about how things currently are, and then complaining ensues.

The moment you permit your mind to dwell with dissatisfaction upon things as they are, you begin to lose ground.

When you fix your attention upon the common, the ordinary, the poor, the squalid and the mean, your mind takes upon itself the form of these things. Then you will transmit these forms or mental images to the formless substance, and the common, the poor, the squalid, and the mean will come to you. To permit your mind to dwell upon the inferior is to become inferior and to surround yourself with inferior things. On the other hand, to fix your attention on the best is to surround yourself with the best, and to become the best. The creative power within us makes us into the image of that which we give our attention to. We are made of thinking substance, and thinking substance always takes the form of that which it thinks about. The grateful mind is constantly fixed upon the best, and therefore it tends to become the best. It takes the form or character of the best and will receive the best.

Faith is born of gratitude. The grateful mind continually expects good things, and that expectation becomes faith. The reaction of gratitude upon one's own mind produces faith and every outgoing wave of grateful thanksgiving increases faith. Those who have no feeling of gratitude cannot long retain a living faith, and without a living faith you cannot get rich by the creative method, as we shall see in the following chapters. It is necessary, then, to cultivate the habit of being grateful for every good thing that comes to you and to give thanks continuously. Because all things have contributed to your advancement, you should include all things in your gratitude.

Do not waste your time thinking or talking about the shortcomings or wrong actions of plutocrats or trust magnates. Their organization of the world so far has made your opportunity, and it is fruitless to try and change things beyond your control. Focus on what you are building.

Do not throw yourself into a rage against corrupt politicians or turmoil about world events far away from you. Acknowledge that you can do nothing to change much but your own actions and your own thoughts. Focus on gratitude and this will bring you into harmony with the good in everything, and the good in everything will move toward and become evident to you.

...but what about all those rich & powerful jerks?

Do not misinterpret the passages in this chapter to mean that you should not stand up for what you believe in or that you have to tolerate things that are done by those in authority positions that are harmful to you or others. I believe what Wattles is saying here is to not allow those things to consume so much of your energy that you get fearful and angry and stay distracted from pursuing your goals and creating the life of your dreams.

*Yes, there are a small number of rich, powerful jerks who do rich, powerful jerk things. What are you going to do about it? React to every breaking news story with rage and fear until you give yourself a panic attack? Glue your eyeballs to the television or your phone so that you don't miss out on every bit of gossip or drama that is being blasted into your face at the speed of light? **Why?** What good is it doing you? Do not waste your life absorbing all that negativity. It isn't worth it, and you're not trying to be like them anyway. Focus on what you want to build and who you want to be instead.*

Especially in this age of hyper-sensationalized news on every device, in every newspaper, on every screen, and distracting everyone on social media, it has never been more important to choose to disconnect from the drama of the outside world and focus on what is right in front of you. Connect more with the people and things that are most important to you and do what you can to make things better by making better things.

When in doubt, stick to gratitude and doing to others what you would have them do to you. It's hard to go wrong with the Golden Rule and being thankful for what you have right where you are as you travel the path.

Fall seven times, stand up eight.

- Japanese proverb -

chapter 8:
thinking in the certain way

To create, receive, or manifest anything, you must first form a clear and definite picture of what you want.

Turn back to chapter 6 and read again the story of the man who formed a mental image of his house, and you will get a fair idea of the initial step toward getting rich. You cannot transmit an idea unless you have it yourself. You must have it before you can give it, and many people fail to draw forth what they imagine from the thinking substance because they have themselves only a vague and misty concept of the things they want to do, have, make, or become.

It is not enough that you should have a general desire for wealth "to do good with" - everybody has that desire. It is not enough that you should have a wish to travel, see things, live more, etc. Everybody has those desires also. If you were going to send a message to a friend, you would not send the letters of the alphabet in their order and let them construct the message for themselves, nor would you list words at random from the dictionary. You would send a coherent sentence – one which meant something and was easy to understand.

When you try to impress your wants upon the formless substance, remember that it must be done by a coherent statement and vision. You must know what you want, and be definite. You can never get rich or set the creative power into action by sending out unformed longings and vague desires.

Meditate on your desires and envision them just as the man I described earlier went over his house in his imagination. Imagine just what you want and get a clear mental picture of it as you wish it to look when you get it.

Keep your clear mental picture continually in your mind, as the sailor has in mind the port toward which he is sailing the ship. You must keep your attention toward it all the time.

You must no more lose sight of your vision than the captain of a ship loses sight of the compass. It is not necessary to take classes in concentration, nor to set apart special times for prayer and affirmation, nor to go into silent mountain retreats, nor to do occult stunts of any kind. All you need is to know what you want and to want it badly enough so that it will stay in your thoughts. Spend as much of your leisure time as you can in contemplating your mental image.

No one needs to take exercises to concentrate their mind on something which they really want. It is the things you do not really care about which require effort to fix your attention upon them. It will hardly be worthwhile for you to try to carry out the instructions given in this book unless you really want to get rich.

The desire to do so must be strong enough to hold your thoughts directed to that purpose - much like the magnetic pole holds the needle of the compass. The methods I offer here are for people whose desire for riches is strong enough to overcome mental laziness and the love of ease, and are ready to put in the work required to achieve those goals. The more clear and definite you make your mental picture then, and the more you dwell upon it, bringing out all its delightful details, the stronger your desire will be. The stronger your desire, the easier it will be to hold your mind fixed upon the picture of what you want. Something more is necessary, however, than merely to see the picture clearly. If that is all you do, you are only a dreamer, and will have little or no power for accomplishment.

Behind your clear vision must be the purpose to realize it and to bring it forth in tangible expression. Behind this purpose must be an invincible and unwavering faith that the thing is already yours. You must believe that it is available for you and that what you imagine is waiting for you to take action and take possession of it.

Envision the new house mentally until it takes form around you physically. In the mental realm, enter at once into full enjoyment of the things you want. Be grateful for what you currently have and for the blessings to come. Imagine your goals realized, and then begin building what you imagine right where you are.

"Whatever things you ask for when you pray, believe that you have received them, and you shall have them," said Jesus. See the things you want as if they were actually around you all the time. See yourself as owning and using them. Make use of them in your imagination just as you will use them when they are your tangible possessions.

Dwell upon your mental picture until it is clear and distinct, and then take the mental attitude of ownership toward everything in that picture. Take possession of it in your mind, in the full faith that it is actually yours. Hold to this mental ownership. Do not waver in doubt and fear. Remember what was said in a proceeding chapter about gratitude – be as thankful for it as you expect to be when it has taken form in your reality.

The person who can sincerely be thankful for the things which are currently only in their imagination has real faith. That person will get rich and can cause the creation of whatsoever they want.

You do not need to pray repeatedly for things that you want. It is not necessary to tell God about it every day. *"Do not use vain repetitions as the heathen do, for your Father knows that you have need of these things before you ask Him,"* said Jesus said to his pupils. Your part is to intelligently articulate and form your desire for the things which make for a larger life, and to arrange your life in a way that makes room for those things to be built or to manifest in your life. It is then that you can impress this whole desire upon the formless substance which has the power and the will to bring you what you want.

You do not make this impression by repeating strings of words over and over. You make it by holding the vision with unshakable **purpose** to attain it, and with steadfast faith that you will attain it. The answer to your prayers do not come according to your faith while you are talking and sitting around, but according to your faith while you are working and building right where you are with a mental posture of restful anticipation. You cannot impress the mind of God by having a special sabbath or holy day set apart to tell him what you want and then forget him during the rest of the week.

You cannot impress God by having special hours to go into your "prayer closet" and pray if you then dismiss the matter from your mind until the hour of prayer comes again. Oral prayer is well enough, and has its effect – especially upon your mind in clarifying your vision and strengthening your faith – but it is not your oral petitions which get you what you want.

In order to get rich, you don't need to set aside some special or dedicated prayer time. You must meditate on and focus on your goals regularly.

By meditate, I mean holding steadily to your vision with the purpose that will cause its creation into solid form and the faith that you are doing so. The whole matter turns on receiving, once you have clearly formed your vision. At this point, it is fine to make an oral statement, addressing God in reverent prayer. From that moment forward, you must envision in your mind what you want and believe that you will receive what you ask for.

Live in the new house. Wear the fine clothes. Ride in the automobile. Go on the journey, and confidently plan for greater journeys. Think and speak of all the things you have asked for in terms of actual present ownership.

Imagine your environment and a financial condition exactly as you want them and live as much as you can in that imaginary environment and financial condition until such time as you are able to build that reality piece by piece until you have realized your goals.

Keep in mind, however, that you do not do this as a mere dreamer and mental castle builder: hold to the faith that the imaginary is being realized, and focus on the purpose for its realization as you build.

Remember that it is faith and purpose in the use of the imagination which make the difference between the scientist and the dreamer.

Having learned this fact, it is in the next chapter that you must learn the proper use of the will.

Tell me what ya want, what ya really, really want

*Stop and think about this for a moment. Have you ever **actually** asked yourself what you really want in this life? So often we get caught up in what we think we need or what our parents, spouses, loved ones, co-workers, friends, family members, teachers, pastors, politicians, or other authority figures want us to do for **them** that we don't think about what we actually want for **ourselves**.*

If you find yourself feeling frustrated and like most of your life just boils down to reacting to what everyone else expects from you, it's no wonder why you're miserable! We all do it. Don't beat yourself up. But its better to recognize it now and start doing something different if you actually want to see that change. You've got to take better care of yourself.

*You cannot "love others as you love yourself" until you first learn to love yourself. This is not a selfish act - it is necessary in order to really achieve lasting happiness and the goals that you have in a sustainable way. Say this out loud and see how doing so makes you feel: "**Self-care is not selfish.**" If you feel any resistance around that, explore why. You might be surprised what you discover. Write down and meditate on the thoughts that come to mind.*

First and foremost, you must figure out what it is that you actually want. Write "What do I really want?" on a big piece of paper and jot down the answers that come to mind. Then hang that piece of paper up next to your bathroom mirror or somewhere that you'll see it every day. It will help illuminate things that you may have set aside out of fear or outside pressure. Just try it and see what happens. What do you have to lose?

Another thing that I have found to be extremely effective is creating a 'vision board'. You can do a simple web search for 'vision board' and see all kinds of examples. It's fun and easy: just get a piece of poster board from a local department or craft store, some magazines, scissors and a glue stick.

There's no wrong way to do this.

Go through the magazines and cut out images and phrases that stand out to you. Glue them on the poster board in whatever order or arrangement that you like. If there are particular images that you find online that inspire you, print those out and use them as well. It could be simple things like encouraging words and phrases or physical items like houses, locations, and objects. I also add to my vision board things that remind me of past successes that I have had: pay stubs from large client gigs that we have landed, receipts for debts that I have paid off, acceptance letters from deals I've pitched, etc. Though it might feel or sound silly and childish if you have never done it, the point of this exercise is to have in your home or office a constant reminder of what you are aiming at as well as reminders of the successes you have already attained.

When things get tough (and they inevitably will at some point), that vision board is something to go back to and remind yourself what you're wanting to do, how you want your life to look, and the struggles you have already overcome. When you know WHY you are doing something, it makes it much easier to handle the HOW. Try it - you won't regret it. My vision boards have often served as mental and emotional anchors when the inevitable storms of life have hit. I am always grateful when those storms are raging that I took the time to create things that help keep me focused on what's important. As I've said before - do not think Wattles is suggesting that you just sit in a room and imagine what you want all day long.

Getting a clear vision of the life you want is of utmost importance - but vision without taking consistent action in the direction of those goals is simply fantasy. Just envisioning what you want is not enough. It is a vital first step - one that many resist doing because they feel it is foolish or childish. But it is not the only step - ***you must take action in the direction of your dreams****...even if that means learning how to position yourself to act and receive the manifestation of those dreams when they begin to come to you. We'll get into that next as we discuss the will.*

Nothing diminishes
anxiety faster
than action.

- Walter Anderson -

chapter 9:
how to use the will

Do not try to apply your will power to anyone outside of yourself. You have no right to do so.

It is wrong to apply your will to other people in order to get them to do what you wish done. It is as flagrantly wrong and unethical to coerce people by mental power as it is to coerce them by physical power. If compelling people by physical force to do things for you is wrong and immoral, attempting to compel them by mental means is immoral also; the only difference is in methods. If taking things from people by physical force is robbery, then taking things by mental force is robbery also. There is no difference in principle. You have no right to use your will power upon another person, even if you believe it is "for their own good," for you do not know what would be good for them. The science of getting rich does not require you to apply power or force to any other person in any way whatsoever. There is not the slightest necessity for doing so. Indeed, any attempt to use your will upon others will only tend to defeat your purpose.

You do not need to apply your will to things in order to compel them to come to you. That would simply be trying to coerce God and would be foolish and useless, as well as irreverent. You do not have to compel God to give you good things any more than you have to use your will power to make the sun rise. You do not have to use your will power to conquer an unfriendly deity, or to make stubborn and rebellious spiritual forces do your bidding. The formless substance is friendly to you and is more willing to give you what you want than you are to get it. To get rich, you need only to use your will power upon yourself.

When you know what to think and do, then you must use your will to compel and discipline yourself to think and do the right things. That is the legitimate use of the will in getting what you want; that is, to use it in holding yourself to the right course of consistent, disciplined action.

Do not try to project your will, your thoughts, or your mind out into space or to act upon other people or external things.

Use your will to keep yourself thinking and acting in the certain way. Keep your mind at home and focused on improving your present environment. It can accomplish more there than elsewhere. Use your mind to form a mental image of what you want and hold to that vision with faith and purpose. Use your will to keep your mind working in this way. The more steady and continuous your faith and purpose, the more rapidly you will get rich, because you will make only positive impressions and thoughts upon your imagination and the world around you, and you will not neutralize or offset your efforts with negative impressions and thoughts.

How you use your attention and what you focus on will determine in many ways the results that you experience. This works both with positive and negative thoughts. Every hour and moment you spend in giving heed to doubts and fears – every hour you spend in worry – and every hour in which your soul is possessed by unbelief will delay the manifestation of what you desire. Since belief is all important, it seriously benefits you to guard your thoughts. As your beliefs will be shaped to a very great extent by the things you observe and think about, it is important that you should command and focus your attention.

Here the will comes into use, for it is by your will that you determine upon what things your attention shall be fixed. If you want to become rich, you must not make a study of poverty. Things are not brought into being by thinking about their opposites.

Health is never to be attained by studying disease and thinking about disease. Righteousness is not promoted by studying sin and thinking about sin, and no one ever got rich by studying poverty and thinking about poverty. Medicine as a science of disease has in many ways increased disease; religion as a science of sin has promoted sin, and economics as a study of poverty will fill the world with wretchedness and want.

Do not talk about poverty. Do not investigate it or concern yourself with it. Never mind what its causes are, as you have nothing to do with them.

What concerns you is the cure.

"If it bleeds, it leads" is terrible advice.

There are countless things that are constantly screaming for your attention. Never before in human history have we all been more connected to one another - and there are truly amazing and wonderful things happening all over the world. At the same time, the mainstream and corporate news media (on both sides of the political spectrum) will often only focus on the sensational, the violent, the fearful, and the dramatic things that are going on because that is how they make their money – by keeping you distracted.

It does not have to be this way. It has perhaps never been more important to learn how to be very intentional and selective in what you feed your mind upon - because what you feed your mind upon will ultimately determine the world view that you adopt and how you conduct yourself. It has often been said "you are what you think" - so choose carefully. There is a big difference between promoting something in a way that informs and entertains your audience about a valuable product or service that you are offering...and blatant, intentional and Machiavellian manipulation for profit and power.

I strongly advise against the latter. It will not make you happy in the long run, and when people realize you've been manipulating them, they will no longer trust you or purchase your products or services. You don't like it when it happens to you - so kindly reconsider when thinking about doing so to others. As mentioned earlier, Lynne Twist's book "The Soul of Money" addresses this topic in great detail and I highly recommend it along with the other books listed at the back of this book.

Do not spend all of your time in typical charitable work, or typical charity movements. Most typical charity work only tends to perpetuate the poverty it aims to eradicate. I do not say that you should be hard hearted or unkind and refuse to hear the cry of need. You must simply not try to eradicate poverty in any of the conventional ways. Put poverty behind you, and put all that pertains to it behind you. **Focus on creating the good.**

Get rich - that is the best way that you can help the poor. What tends to do away with poverty is not getting pictures of poverty into your mind, but conveying the idea of riches into the minds of the poor.

You cannot hold to the mental image which will make you rich if you fill your mind with pictures of poverty. Do not focus on books, articles or papers which give circumstantial accounts of the wretchedness of the tenement dwellers, of the horrors of child labor, and so on. Do not meditate upon anything which fills your mind with gloomy images of want and suffering. You cannot help the poor in the least by focusing upon all of these things. The wide-spread knowledge of them does not tend at all to do away with poverty.

You are not deserting the poor in their misery when you refuse to allow your mind to be filled with pictures of that misery. Poverty can be done away with - not by increasing the number of well-to-do people who think and focus on poverty - but by increasing the number of poor people who set out with faith and purpose to get rich via the creative and scientific method and rise out of their poverty.

The poor do not need charity - they need inspiration. A lot of charity only sends them a loaf of bread to keep them alive in their poverty or gives them entertainment to make them forget for an hour or two. Inspiration will cause them to want to rise out of their misery. If you want to help the poor, demonstrate to them that they can become rich. You can prove it by getting rich yourself. The only way in which poverty will ever be banished from this world is by getting a large and constantly increasing number of people to learn how to create wealth for themselves and their loved ones by the creative method.

People must be taught to become rich by creation, not by competition.

Every person who becomes rich by competition throws down behind them the ladder by which they rose and keeps others down. On the contrary, every person who gets rich by the creative method opens a way for many others to follow them and inspires multitudes to do so.

You are not showing hardness of heart or an unfeeling disposition when you refuse to pity poverty, focus on poverty, read about poverty, think or talk about it, or to listen to those who do talk endlessly about it. Use your will power to keep your mind OFF the subject of poverty, and to keep it fixed with faith and purpose ON the vision of what you want and the creative method of getting rich.

Your focus will determine your future.

There are amazing charities all over the world doing great work for those in need - and if you truly desire to work with or start an organization to help others, awesome! That means you have a soul and that's a good thing. If you are interested in helping people out of poverty, my encouragement would be to do so in a way that empowers and educates them in harnessing the creative process and teach them how to leverage their focus and attention to get out of their poverty. What Wattles is saying in this chapter is that unless you plan to go into that kind of work, the best thing you can do is make sure that your own household is well taken care of before you go about trying to help others or stressing out over all the horror-stories in the news.

This is an issue of "loving your neighbor as you love yourself" - you must love yourself first. Think of it in the same way that you must first put your own oxygen mask on during an in-flight emergency before you can help someone else. By filling your mind with possibility, inspiration, hope, faith, and then demonstrating that you can rise out of your own financial troubles, you pave the way for countless others who will see your example. Get your own financial situation sorted out. Get rich by the creative method - and then focus on empowering others to do the same later if that's your desire.

Also, do not take from this chapter that Wattles is suggesting you should stick your head in the sand about very real issues and important events going on in the world and in your community. What I believe he is saying is to get a healthy dose of perspective when it comes to the prevailing world view that you hold. Focus on what you can actually control: you.

Put simply, if you believe the world is falling apart, you will act accordingly...even if that is not actually true.

On the flip side, if your attention is on the good, the true, the peaceful, the encouraging, and the hopeful things in your world, your mood will be better, your actions will be much more positive, and you can focus more on creating a better world for you and your loved ones.

If there is a cause that you truly care about and you feel that there are stories that need to be told or voices that need to be heard, then do your part to share and amplify them. Of course there are things about the world that you wish were different! **The question then becomes – what are you going to do about it?**

Ask yourself if the things you are focusing on are within or outside of your control...and act accordingly. Don't get so caught up in the for-profit drama that bombards us each day in the media that you lose sight of the fact that you can create positive change where you are and that you can start now.

Henry Ford supposedly said, "Whether you think you can, or think you can't, you're right." If he did say that, this is coming from a guy who disrupted the entire horse and buggy method of transportation with his automobiles! He likely would not have done all the things that he did if he believed the world was ending like many were saying even in his day.

The doomsday prophets and sensationalist fear-mongers have always been around - and likely always will be. They prey on people's fear to enrich themselves. The number of times they have been wrong with their end-of-the-world predictions has far exceeded any times they were right...and even a broken clock is right twice a day.

Prove them wrong again. **Create something better.**

Don't find fault.
Find a solution.

- Henry Ford -

chapter 10:
further use of the will

You cannot retain a true and clear vision of wealth if you are constantly turning your attention to negative imagery or ideas, whether they be external or imaginary.

Do not complain about your past troubles of a financial nature. If you have had them, do not waste your creative energy thinking about them at all except as something you have chosen to move on from. Do not complain about the poverty of your parents or the hardships of your early life. To do any of these things is to mentally class yourself with the poor or for the time being, and it will certainly slow the movement of things in your direction. At the very least, you will present yourselves to others as a victim of circumstance and whether this is true or not, many people have their own challenges and to complain about yours does not help you move forward.

"Let the dead bury their dead," as Jesus said.

Put poverty and all things that pertain to poverty completely behind you. You have accepted a certain theory of the universe as being correct, and are resting all your hopes of happiness on its being correct. What can you gain by giving heed to conflicting theories?

Do not read religious books which tell you that the world is soon coming to an end, and do not read the writing or listen to the ravings of fear-mongers, naysayers, and pessimistic doom-and-gloom philosophers who tell you that the world is going to the devil. The world is not going to the devil, it is going to God. It is wonderful becoming.

Yes, there may be a good many things and existing conditions which are disagreeable and upsetting, but what is the use of studying them when they are passing away and when the study of them only tends to delay their passing and keep them with us? Why give time and attention to things which are being removed by evolutionary growth when you can hasten their removal only by speeding up that process of making things better as far as your part of it goes?

No matter how horrible conditions in certain countries, areas, or other places seem to be, you waste your time by focusing on them. You should interest yourself in the world's becoming rich. Think of the riches the world is coming into instead of the poverty it is growing out of. Keep in mind that the only way in which you can assist the world in growing rich is by growing rich yourself through the creative method, not the competitive one.

Give your attention wholly to creating riches and do not focus on poverty.

Whenever you think or speak of those who are poor, think and speak of them as those who are waiting to be empowered to become rich - as those who simply need to be educated rather than pitied. Then they and others will be inspired and begin to search for the way out. Because I say that you are to give your whole time and mind and thought to riches, it does not follow that you are to be cruel or mean.

To become really rich is the noblest aim you can have in life, for it includes everything else. On the competitive plane, the struggle to get rich is a godless scramble for power over other people, but when we come into the creative mind, all this is changed. All that is possible in the way of greatness, soul unfoldment, service and lofty endeavor comes by way of getting rich. All is made possible by the use of things. If you lack for physical health, you will find that the attainment of it is conditional on your getting rich.

Only those who are set free from financial worry and who have the means to live a care-free existence and follow hygienic practices can have and retain true health. Moral and spiritual greatness and wealth is possible only to those who rise above the competitive battle for existence. Only those who are becoming rich on the plane of creative thought are free from the destructive influences of competition.

This section may strike a nerve or twelve.

*This section will especially ring true if you have ever been in financial circumstances where you have worried about whether or not you are going to be able to pay rent, keep food on the table, or pay for medical treatment if you get sick or injured. It is **very** difficult to think about anything else if you aren't sure that your basic needs will be met. That is the gist of what Wattles is getting at in this chapter so far. Without your physical, emotional, and financial needs taken care of, it becomes very hard to function at all.*

*Whether we like it or not, having an abundance of finances to handle the issues of life makes dealing with them much simpler. It is better to focus on acknowledging this fact and get on with the work of making it happen instead of getting into fruitless debates about whether or not "getting rich" is a good idea. The idea that there is more than enough for everyone can be hard to comprehend when we have all been so conditioned to function from a mentality of lack versus a mentality of abundance. **You must choose to believe it before you will experience it as a reality and before you can act on this fact.***

Also, regardless of your personal religious beliefs, let's talk about the concept of 'faith' for a moment. Your 'faith' mindset is key. Either you choose to have faith, believe in, and focus on the things that are getting better in this world or you choose to have faith, believe in, and focus on the things that are getting worse. Your choice here will ultimately define the kind of life that you live, the actions you take, and the results you see. If you believe the world is falling apart, you'll act like it and your world will seem like it is falling apart. Your perspective is a choice.

If the stories you've been telling yourself around money and happiness aren't working out for you, what would it look like to tell yourself a different story for a change?

If your heart is set on domestic happiness, remember that love flourishes best where there is refinement, a high level of thought, and freedom from corrupting influences. These are to be found only where riches are attained by the exercise of creative thought, without strife or rivalry. I repeat, you can aim at nothing so great or noble as to become rich. You must fix your attention upon your mental picture of riches to the exclusion of all thoughts or theories that may tend to dim or obscure that vision.

You must learn to see the underlying truth in all things. You must see beneath all seemingly wrong conditions that there is the great one life ever moving forward toward fuller expression and more complete happiness. It is the truth that there is no such thing as poverty - there is only wealth. Some people remain in poverty because they are ignorant of the fact that there is wealth for them. These people can best be taught by showing them the way to affluence in your own person and practice.

Some are poor because while they feel that there is a way out, they are too intellectually lazy to put forth the mental effort necessary to find that way and travel by it. For these, the very best thing you can do is to arouse their desire by showing them the happiness that comes from getting rich via the creative method, not the competitive one. Others still are poor because, while they have some notion of science, they have become so swamped and lost in the maze of metaphysical and occult theories that they do not know which road to take. They try a mixture of many systems and fail in all. For these, again, the best thing to do is to show the right way in your own person and practice.

An ounce of doing things is worth a pound of theorizing.

The very best thing you can do for the whole world is to make the most of yourself. You can serve God and humanity most effectively by getting rich. That is, if you get rich by the creative method and not by the competitive one. I assert that this book gives in detail the principles of the science of getting rich. If that is true, you do not need to read any other book upon the subject.

This may sound narrow and egotistical, but consider that there is no more scientific method of computation in mathematics than by addition, subtraction, multiplication, and division; no other method is possible.

There can be but one shortest distance between two points. There is only one way to think scientifically, and that is to think in the way that leads by the most direct and simple route to the goal. No one has yet formulated a briefer or less complex "system" than the one set forth in this book. It has been stripped of all non-essentials. When you begin doing this, lay all others aside - put them out of your mind altogether.

Read this book every day. Keep it with you, commit it to memory, and do not think about other "systems" and theories. If you do, you may begin to have doubts and to be uncertain in your thoughts and actions, and then you will begin to make failures. After you have made good and become rich, you may study other systems as much as you please; but until you are quite sure that you have gained what you want, do not read anything on this subject but this book.

Focus only on the most optimistic comments on the world's news: those in harmony with your mental vision.

Postpone or abandon your investigations into the occult. Do not dabble in theosophy, spiritualism, or kindred studies. It is very likely that the dead still live and are near - but if they are, let them alone.

Mind your own business. Wherever the spirits of the dead may be, they have their own work to do, and their own problems to solve. We have no right to interfere with them. We cannot help them, and it is very doubtful whether they can help us, or whether we have any right to trespass upon their time if they can.

Let the dead and the hereafter alone, and solve your own problems here and now by getting rich. If you begin to mix with the occult or other strange methods, you will start mental cross-currents which will likely bring your hopes to shipwreck.

Perhaps a bit too much bravado and woo?

*As I have stated, I am not as dogmatic about the philosophies in this book (or anything for that matter) as Wattles was. We can get easily distracted by arguing about religion, dogma, and our beliefs about what happens after this life as well as our beliefs about the life we have. The fact is that none of us really know for sure and it is fruitless to debate about these things. Life is much more peaceful when I leave these matters to each individual instead of feeling like it is my responsibility to save anyone or tell someone else what to believe. We all grew up with a wide variety of beliefs about money, politics, and spirituality – and most of it just leads to arguments anyway. I'll keep saying it: **focus on what you can be sure of, what you can control, and what you can create.***

The key to not getting tripped up in this chapter is in seeing that Wattles is drawing our attention to the fact that there is a wealth of abundant resources and solutions to problems all over the planet. When we embrace the creative process over the competitive one, we will find ways to work together and tap into the riches and resources that are all around us. Can you imagine what would happen if the fossil fuel industry would work WITH those who are trying to create cleaner, more sustainable energy solutions instead of trying to keep things the way they have been for so long? Or if higher education institutions took the initiative to fix the student debt problem? Or if the pharmaceutical industries actually were in the business of health and wellness instead of focusing so much on profit at all costs?

*My biggest encouragement with any information that you consume is to take what is useful for you and discard the rest. Test everything with your own experiences. Don't just believe things because some authority figure told you to. The point of "science" is to test it out and see what works for you in practice, yes? Bottom line: don't get so caught up on some of the overly confident sections of this book - **keep your attention on what you can do here and now.***

Now, this and the preceding chapters have brought us to the following statement of basic facts:

- There is a thinking stuff from which all things are made, and which, in its original state, permeates, penetrates, and fills the empty spaces of the universe.

- A thought in this substance produces the thing that is imagined by the thought.

- Humanity can form things in their thoughts, and by impressing their thoughts upon formless substance can cause the things they think about to be created.

- In order to do this, humanity must pass from the competitive to the creative mind.

- You must form a clear mental picture of the things you want. Hold this picture in your thoughts with the fixed purpose to get what you want and the unwavering faith that you will get what you want, closing your mind against all that may tend to shake your purpose, dim your vision, or quench your faith.

- In addition to all of this, we shall now see that you must live and **act** in a certain way.

I am convinced all of humanity is born with more gifts than we know.

Most are born geniuses and just get de-geniused rapidly.

- Buckminster Fuller -

chapter 11:
acting in the certain way

Thought is the initial impelling force that inspires the creative power to act. Thinking in a certain way will start the process of bringing riches to you, but you must not rely on thought alone. You must TAKE ACTION.

This is the rock upon which many otherwise scientific metaphysical thinkers meet shipwreck - *the failure to connect thought with personal action.* We have not yet reached the stage of human development, (even supposing such a stage to be possible), in which we can create directly from the formless substance without nature's processes or the work of human hands.

You must not only think in a certain way, but your personal actions must align with your thoughts.

By thought you can begin the process of causing riches to be impelled toward you, but it will not mine itself, refine itself, or turn itself into coins that come rolling along the road until they bounce their way into your pockets. Humanity's affairs may be so ordered that someone will be led to mine the riches for you, and other people's business transactions may be so inspired that the riches will be brought toward you in various ways and for various reasons – but you must so arrange your own business and financial affairs so that you may be able to receive what you desire. Your thoughts will work to begin to bring you what you want...but your personal actions must be such that you can actually receive what you want when it comes near to you.

You must give every person more in use value than they give you in cash value. You are not to take it as charity, nor to steal it.

The scientific use of thought consists in forming a clear and distinct mental image of what you want. You must hold fast to your reasons for getting what you want, believe with grateful faith that you will get it, and take action accordingly. Do not try to project your thoughts in any mysterious or occult way with the idea of having them go out and do things for you. That is wasted effort and will weaken your power to think and act with clarity and focus.

The function and purpose of thought in getting rich is explained in the preceding chapters. Your faith and purpose positively impresses your vision upon the formless substance, which has the same desire for more life that you have. This vision, received from you, sets all the creative forces at work in and through their regular channels of action, but directed toward you. It is not your role to guide or supervise the creative process - all you have to do with that is retain your vision, stick to your purpose, and maintain your faith and gratitude.

You must act in a certain way so that you can steward what is yours when it comes to you and so that you can receive the things you have in your mental picture and put them in their proper places as they arrive. You can really see the truth of this. When things reach you, they will be in the hands of other people who will ask an equivalent for them. You can only get what is yours by giving the other person what is theirs.

This is the crucial point in the science of getting rich: what you choose to do with this present moment, where thought and personal action must be combined.

Your pocketbook is not going to be transformed magically into a limitless supply which will be always full of money without effort on your part. There are many people who (consciously or unconsciously) set the creative forces in action by the strength and persistence of their desires, but who remain poor because they do not adequately prepare to receive the thing they want when it comes.

You have to say yes to your own success.

Plain and simple - "acting in the certain way" boils down to taking action on the vision that you have for yourself and the life that you desire, right here and right now. It is not your responsibility to try and force something to happen that is the job of someone else (as he mentioned not trying to 'project' your thoughts in a mysterious or occult way). It IS your responsibility to do everything you can with what you have right where you are in order to see and manifest the fulfillment of your goals and dreams.

No one else is going to give you permission to do so. *In fact, you may face some of the most intense resistance from people in your own family or from close "friends" who for one reason or another may be intimidated by your creative pursuits or the thought of your success. You have to give yourself permission to say yes to your own success and to your increasing life. That includes learning how to recognize and define your own value and figuring out ways to ensure that you are receiving what you are due for any creative work that you make or perform for someone else. This can also apply to practical matters like creating marketing plans for your product or service, implementing systems to help you work more efficiently, networking with business partners, seeking mentors, filling out applicable paperwork, business registrations, and setting up business bank accounts if you are finally ready to take your entrepreneurship journey seriously.*

It may feel tedious, overwhelming, and unnecessary, but it's best to set things up right from the start so that you keep good records and see your progress over time. Make sure to look into local credit unions - they often have much better options for small businesses than big banks. Check out software for helping to stay on top of your finances. Do a web search for your local Small Business Development Center - they often have free classes for new and aspiring business owners and are great places to connect with others who are on the path with you. "Acting in the certain way" is all about how you position yourself in alignment with the goals you are pursuing.

Through the power of thought, the thing you want is brought into your consciousness and towards you. It is by action that you receive it.

Whatever actions you choose to take, it is evident that you must act NOW. You cannot act in the past, and it is essential to the clearness of your mental vision that you dismiss the past from your mind. You cannot act in the future, for the future is not here yet. You cannot know exactly how you will want to act in any future contingency until that contingency has arrived. Because you are not in the right business or the right environment now, do not think that you must postpone action until you get into the perfect business or environment.

Do not waste time in the present worrying about how to handle possible future emergencies: have faith in your ability to meet any emergency when it arrives. If you act in the present with your mind on the future, your present actions will be with a divided mind and will not be effective.

Put your whole mind into present action.

Do not put your thoughts out into the world and then sit around and wait for results to just magically arrive. If you do, you will never get anywhere. Act now. There is never any time but now, and there never will be any time but now. If you are ever to begin to prepare for the reception of what you want, you must begin now. The action you take, whatever it is, must be in your present business or employment, and must be with the persons and things in your present environment. You cannot act where you are not. You cannot act where you have been, and you cannot act where you are going to be. You can act only where you are.

Do not overanalyze as to whether yesterday's work was well done or not; do today's work well. Do not try to do tomorrow's work now; there will be plenty of time to do that when you get to it. Do not try by occult or mystical means to act on people or things that are out of your reach or control. Do not wait for a change of environment before you act - get a change of environment by action. You can act upon the environment in which you are now to cause yourself to be transferred to a better environment. Hold in mind with faith and purpose the vision of yourself in the better environment, but act upon your present environment with all your heart, with all your strength, and with all your mind.

Do not waste your time just day dreaming or castle building; hold to the vision of what you want, and act NOW. Do not go about seeking some new thing to do or some strange, unusual, or remarkable action to perform as a first step toward getting rich. It is probable that your actions, at least for some time to come, will be similar to those you have been doing for awhile. Realize that you are to begin now to perform your daily actions in the certain way which will make you rich.

If you are engaged in some kind of business and feel that it is not the right one for you, do not wait until you get into the perfect business before you begin to act. Do not feel discouraged or sit down and lament because you are misplaced. No person was ever so misplaced that they could not find the right place, and no person ever became so involved in the wrong business that they could not get into the right business.

Hold the mental vision of yourself in the right business with the purpose and faith that you will get into it and are getting into it, but ACT in your present business and location.

Use your present business as the stepping stone of getting into a better one, and use your present environment as the means of getting into a better one.

Your vision of the right business, if held with faith and purpose, will cause the supreme power to move the right business toward you. Your actions, if performed in a certain way, will cause you to move toward that business. If you are an employee or wage earner and feel that you must change places in order to get what you want, do not project your thoughts into space and rely upon that to get you another job. It will probably fail to do so. Hold the vision of yourself in the job you want while you ACT with faith and purpose in the job you have and you will get the job you want. Your vision and faith will set creative forces in motion to bring something better toward you, and your action will cause the forces in your own environment to move you toward the place you want. This could include looking for work elsewhere – but you must be the one to do the looking.

You must be the one to take action.

In closing this chapter, we will add another statement to our syllabus:

- There is a thinking stuff from which all things are made, and which, in its original state, permeates, penetrates, and fills the empty spaces of the universe.

- A thought in this substance produces the thing that is imagined by the thought.

- Humanity can form things in their thoughts, and by impressing their thoughts upon formless substance can cause the things they think about to be created.

- In order to do this, humanity must pass from the competitive to the creative mind.

- You must form a clear mental picture of the things you want. Hold this picture in your thoughts with the fixed purpose to get what you want and the unwavering faith that you will get what you want, closing your mind against all that may tend to shake your purpose, dim your vision, or quench your faith.

- So that you may receive what you want when it comes, you must act **NOW** upon and with the people and things in your present environment.

You are here...so whatcha gonna do about it?

*This is the part of the book that really kicked my butt into high gear - because it helped me realize how much of my energy was being wasted **wishing** for something to change instead of actually **doing** something that would cause change to happen. How often have you been in crappy situations or environments and rather than taking practical action to DO something about it, you instead wasted your time and energy wallowing in your misery, complaining to friends/co-workers/family members, and generally just staying stuck in your self-loathing? I don't know about you, but I can certainly attest to getting stuck there over the years! It can sometimes feel more comfortable to stay there in our stuff than to do the deep work and ask ourselves why we aren't taking action (hint: it's usually fear). As Robert Frost said, "The best way out is always through."*

***Do you hate your job?** Have you actually looked and applied elsewhere or are you just mentally disqualifying yourself before you start? Feeling frustrated with that client that is always more trouble than they're worth? Have you considered finding ways to let them go and make more money elsewhere for less hassle? Have you committed to working on that side hustle idea yet? You can start creating better situations for yourself today that will ultimately lead to improved situations in the future. Nobody ever said this was easy – just that it works!*

One thing that helps cultivate a more creative, fulfilling life is to intentionally set up an environment that makes doing your creative work easy.** The key is making it simple for you to practice daily and "get in the zone." Want to be a better musician? Set up your instrument in a more prominent location in your home and play it at least ten minutes a day. Want to be a better writer? Get a journal and write for at least ten minutes every morning when you wake up and for ten minutes before you go to sleep. Just ten minutes! What do you have to lose? So much of the "success" we seek really boils down to one thing: **intentional self-discipline and taking action now.

Life shrinks or expands in proportion to one's courage.

- Anaïs Nin -

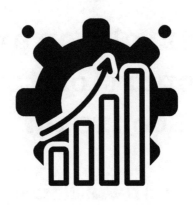

chapter 12:
efficient action

You must use your thought as directed in previous chapters, and begin to do what you can do where you are - and you must do ALL that you can do where you are in an efficient manner.

You can advance only by being larger than your present place and no person is larger than their present place who leaves undone any of the work pertaining to that place. The world is advanced only by those who more than fill their present places. If no person quite filled their present place, you can see that everything would start to regress backwards. Those who do not quite fill their present places are a weight upon society, government, commerce, and industry. They must be carried along by others at a great expense.

The progress of the world is hindered only by those who do not fill the places they are holding. No society could advance if every person was smaller than their place. Social evolution is guided by the law of physical and mental evolution. In the animal world, evolution is caused by excess of life. When an organism has more life than can be expressed in the functions of its own plane, it develops the organs of a higher plane, and a new species is originated. There never would have been new species had there not been organisms which more than filled their places and grew out of them.

The law is exactly the same for you. Getting rich depends upon your applying this principle to your own affairs and business. Every day is either a successful day or a day of failure, and it is the successful days which get you what you want. If everyday is a failure, you can never get rich. On the contrary, if every day is a success, you cannot fail to get rich.

Every day, do all that can be done that day – but remember it is not the number of things you do, but the EFFICIENCY of each action that counts.

If there is something that may be done today and you do not do it, you have failed in so far as that thing is concerned and the consequences may be more disastrous than you yet imagine. You cannot foresee the results of even the most trivial act. You do not know the workings of all the forces that have been set moving on your behalf. Much may be depending on your doing some simple act that may be the very thing which will open the door of opportunity to great possibilities and opportunities.

You can never know all the combinations which the supreme intelligence is making for you in the world of things and of human affairs. Your neglect or failure to do some small thing today may cause a long delay in getting what you want. There is, however, a limitation or qualification of the above that you must take into account.

You are not to overwork, nor to rush blindly into your business in the effort to do the greatest possible number of things in the shortest possible time. Do not to try to do tomorrow's work today, nor to do a week's work in a day. Again: it is not about the number of things you do, but the efficiency of each action that counts.

Every act is, in itself, either a success or a failure. Every act is, in itself, either effective or inefficient. Every inefficient act is a failure, and if you spend your life doing inefficient acts, your whole life will be a failure. The more things you do, the worse for you if all your acts are inefficient ones. On the other hand, every efficient act is a success in itself. If every act of your life is an efficient one, your whole life MUST be a success.

The cause of failure is doing too many things in an inefficient, distracted way instead of an efficient, focused way.

You will see that it is a self-evident proposition that if you do not do any inefficient acts but instead do a sufficient number of efficient acts, you will become rich. If it is possible for you to make each act an efficient one, you see again that the getting of riches is reduced to an exact science, like mathematics.

The 80/20 rule & efficient action

If you are not familiar with it already, do a web search for "the 80/20 principle". This is also known as the Pareto Principle and it states that about 80% of the results you get come from 20% of the actions you are taking. For example in sports training, roughly 20% of certain exercises and eating habits have 80% of the impact in the athlete's overall fitness. Author and investor Tim Ferriss will often use the phrase "the minimum effective dose" when discussing those actions that, if taken consistently over time, will produce the desired results much faster.

It requires a good bit of self-awareness to pay attention to how you are using your time and energy, but if you do an 80/20 analysis of your actions, you will discover quickly where most of your results are coming from. If you are spending 80% of your 'free time' binging on Netflix or some other form of mindless entertainment like web browsing or social media instead of building your creative skill set, chances are high that you won't achieve the results you want very quickly. Approximately 80% of my income and opportunities come from 20% of my network. Many business owners will acknowledge this spread is fairly accurate for their own pursuits. Knowing this, I can more intentionally cultivate better relationships with that 20% group to maximize my chances for future success and new possibilities.

*If you have been an employee of someone else for the majority of your life up to this point, one of the most difficult battles you will face is learning how to be more self-directed in your goal-setting and income generation as opposed to having someone tell you what to do all day long. If you want freedom from the 9-5 cubicle lifestyle, you'll need to learn how to master and use your time and energy when you're not at work in the direction of pursuing what you really want. Why? Because once you don't have a boss to give you orders anymore, you'll be the boss of your own time and energy! With that comes challenges that many people don't know how to navigate... yet. **The best time to start learning is now - so kudos to you, champ.***

Every act can be made strong and efficient by meditating on your vision while you are taking action and putting the whole power of your faith and purpose into THIS moment.

The matter turns, then, on the question of whether you can make each separate act a success in itself, and this you can certainly do. You can make each act a success because the supreme power is working with you and the supreme power cannot fail. The supreme power is at your service. Every action is either strong or weak. When every action is strong, efficient, and focused, you are acting in the certain way which will make you rich. To make each act efficient, you have only to put your own creativity, presence, and willpower into it.

It is at this point that many people fail to separate mental power from personal action. They use the power of their mind in one place and at one time but they take action in another place and at another time. They are "mentally time traveling." Their acts are not successful in themselves and many of them are inefficient.

Remember that successful action is cumulative in its results. Since the desire for more life is inherent in all things, when you begin to move toward a larger and more expressive life, more opportunities are drawn to you and the influence of your desire is multiplied. If you welcome the supreme creative power into every act no matter how commonplace, every act will be a success in itself. As in the nature of things, every success opens the way to other successes. In this way, your progress towards what you want and the speed of what you want coming towards you will become increasingly rapid.

Again - do all that you can do each day and do each act in an efficient, focused manner.

In saying that you must hold your vision while you are doing each act, however trivial or commonplace, I do not mean to say that it is necessary at all times to see the vision distinctly to its smallest details. It should be the work of your leisure hours to use your imagination on the details of your vision and to contemplate them until they are firmly fixed in your mind. If you wish speedy results, use as much time as you can in this practice of intentional meditation, then take action.

By continuous contemplation, you will get the picture of what you want firmly fixed upon your mind, even to the smallest details. This will be transferred to the mind of the formless substance. In your working hours, you need only to mentally refer to your picture to stimulate your faith and purpose and cause your best effort to be put forth.

Remember why you got started and it becomes easier to keep going. Contemplate your picture in your leisure hours until your consciousness is so full of it that you can grasp it instantly. You will become so enthused with its bright promises that the mere thought of it will call forth the strongest energies of your whole being.

Let us again repeat our syllabus, and by slightly changing the closing statements bring it to the point we have now reached.

- There is a thinking stuff from which all things are made, and which, in its original state, permeates, penetrates, and fills the empty spaces of the universe.

- A thought in this substance produces the thing that is imagined by the thought.

- Humanity can form things in their thoughts, and by impressing their thoughts upon formless substance can cause the things they think about to be created.

- In order to do this, humanity must pass from the competitive to the creative mind.

- You must form a clear mental picture of the things you want, and do, with faith and purpose, all that can be done each day to achieve that goal, doing each separate thing in an efficient manner.

- You must act **NOW** upon the people and things in your present environment.

You must choose to be here, now.

Think about it - how much of your thought energy is wasted worrying about the future, regretting the past, and ignoring or avoiding the present moment? These frustrating thought gymnastics can be described as a form of "mental time travel" and they aren't just a minor irritant. They will slow down or outright sabotage the pursuit of your dreams. ***If you find yourself mentally time traveling, slow down and take a few deep breaths. Now say to yourself, "this is not useful" - and move on.*** *The only way you will accomplish your goals is by putting your energy and focus on the present moment, the things you can do and control, and taking action today.*

You can 'act now upon the people and things in your present environment' in practical ways by adding to your vision board, visiting new places that inspire you, organizing your creative or work space, getting rid of old things that don't bring you joy, making something new, and spending time with people who champion you and your goals. Do not waste your time or sabotage your creative spark and energy by hanging around people who just drag you down or by consuming information that just leaves you feeling fearful and hopeless. It will not help you achieve your goals and will surely delay your achieving them.

Another note here on the "formless substance" term - one way to look at it is as your subconscious. What you focus on and think about will grow in your mind and the thoughts you ruminate and meditate on will often be the ones you end up acting (or not acting) upon in one form or another. You can also 'contemplate your picture' by looking regularly at your notes, your vision boards, and things you hang up around your home or office to keep you inspired and focused. Creating an environment that fuels your creativity is a major key to transforming your perspective on the world around you.

...and if you're looking for some inspirational art swag or home decor, make sure to check out my shop @ RDShop.biz !

It is not the mountain that we conquer, but ourselves.

- Sir Edmund Hillary -

chapter 13: getting into the right business

Success in any particular business depends upon your possessing the necessary mindsets, wisdom, connections, and mastering the skills that are required in that business arena.

Without good musical skills, it should be obvious that no one can succeed as a teacher of music. Without well-developed mechanical skills, no one can achieve great success in any of the mechanical trades. Without tact, good relationships, and an understanding of commerce, no one can succeed in their business pursuits.

Merely possessing the skills required in your particular vocation does not ensure getting rich. There are musicians who have remarkable talent and who yet remain poor. There are engineers, artists, and so on who have excellent technical and mechanical ability but who do not get rich. There are business people with certain skills in some areas who nevertheless fail at getting rich. The different skills you can learn are tools for the journey. It is essential to have good tools, but it is also essential that the tools should be used in the right way. This happens through practice, patience, and dedicating yourself to mastering your craft.

One person can take a sharp saw, a square, a good plane, and so on and build a handsome piece of furniture. Another person can take the same tools and get to work to duplicate the piece, but their final production will be a failure. Why? That person does not know how to use their tools or skills in a successful way. The various faculties of your mind and your skill set are the tools with which you must do the work that will make you rich. It will be easier for you to succeed if you get into a business for which you are well equipped with the right mental tools.

"We don't need no education..."

How you define "success" is subjective and depends on the skills you choose to cultivate over time. Don't think for a moment that if you desire to learn how to do something but don't feel "gifted" at it that you cannot teach yourself how to do whatever that thing is. No musician ever started out being an amazing musician. No artist ever started out being great at painting. It all takes practice - lots, and lots, and lots of practice. You didn't know how to walk on day one out of the womb. Art, business, and success are the same way. You must practice regularly and stop looking at learning like it is somewhere that you arrive. It is a life-long journey.

If you want to do something and don't know how to do it, put in the work and learn! Don't wait around for the universe to just magically bestow these gifts upon you. It is work and practice over time that brings excellence and success in any endeavor. It is not luck or inherent "I-was-born-with-it" talent. You must CHOOSE to learn and then PRACTICE new things.

You must shift from obligation-based, school-style education into deciding to cultivate a life of intentional, choice-based learning. That means you get to pick what you want to learn and nobody is going to tell you what to do or how to do it. There is no grade or test to pass. There is simply a life-long path before you where you can choose to become who you want to be and step into the life that you truly want. It will take effort, a lot of trial and error, and daily practice. It's not glamorous or a competition and it will take time before you start seeing results...but it works and it's worth it!

You can learn just about anything for FREE with the internet or in your local library. An excellent book on the topic of cultivating daily learning and creative habits is "The Practice" by Seth Godin. Make sure to utilize the additional resources & recommended reading at the end of this book to help you on your journey. Don't believe the lie that you can't learn new things. You must simply cultivate the willpower to do so and put in the work.

No one should think of their career or current skill set as being irrevocably fixed by the gifts or predisposition with which they were born.

Generally speaking, you will do best in a business that will use your strongest skills for which you may be naturally "best fitted," but there are limitations to this statement. You can get rich in ANY business, for if you do not have the right talent for your particular desired business, you can develop and improve that talent. It merely means that you will have to learn new skills and acquire or make the proper tools and relationships as you go along instead of confining yourself to the use of those with which you were born or which are presently available.

You will get rich most easily if you do something for which you are best fitted, but you will get rich most satisfactorily if you do something that you WANT to do.

It will be EASIER for you to succeed in a vocation for which you already have the talents or skills in a well-developed state, but you CAN succeed in any vocation. You can learn and develop any rudimentary talent or skill over time with practice and focused intention.

Doing what you want to do when you are free from obligations is life-giving. There is no real satisfaction in living if we are compelled to be forever doing something which we do not like to do and can never do what we want to do. It is certain that you can do what you want to do - the desire to do it is proof that you have within you the power to do it.

Desire is a manifestation of power.

Think of the desire to play music like it is an innate, undeveloped power within you that is seeking expression and development. Think of the desire to invent mechanical devices or new technologies as if those things seeking expression and development through you. Where there is no power to do a thing, either developed or undeveloped, there is never any desire to do that thing. Where there is strong desire to do a thing, it is proof that the power to do so is strong and only requires to be developed and applied in the right way.

You are under no true obligation to do what you do not like to do. You should not do those things except as a means to bring you to a place where you are doing what you want to do.

All things otherwise being equal, it is best to select the business for which you have the best developed talent. However, if you have a strong desire to engage in any particular line of work, you should select that work as your main goal. You can do what you want to do, and because of that, it is your right and privilege to pursue the business or vocation which will be most desirable and pleasant. If there are past mistakes whose consequences have placed you in an undesirable business or environment, you may be obliged for some time to do what you do not like to do, but you can make the present moment more pleasant by choosing to take actions today that will start you on the road to be doing what you want to do.

If you feel that you are not in the right vocation, do not act too hastily in trying to get into another one. Generally, the best way to change your business or environment is through personal and professional growth. If you don't like where you are, begin looking for new work while currently employed. You are under no obligation to tell your current employer that you are seeking work elsewhere. Doing so will likely make your present environment and experience of it worse. Do not be afraid to make a sudden and radical change if a better opportunity is presented and you feel after careful consideration that it is the right opportunity. However, never take sudden or radical action when you are in doubt as to the wisdom of doing so and lacking internal peace.

There is never any hurry on the creative plane, and there is no lack of opportunity. In times of doubt and indecision, cultivate gratitude.

Once you get out of the competitive mindset, you will understand that you never need to act hastily. No one else is going to beat you to the thing you want to do. There is more than enough for all. If one space is taken, another and a better one will be opened for you a little farther on.

When you are in doubt, wait. There is plenty of time and hurry does not help you.

Fall back on the contemplation of your vision and increase your faith and purpose. Again and by all means, **in times of doubt and indecision, cultivate gratitude.**

A day or two spent contemplating the vision of what you want and in earnest thanksgiving that you are getting it will bring your mind into such close relationship with the supreme power that you will make no mistake when you do act.

There is a mind which knows all there is to know, and you can come into close unity with this mind by faith and the purpose to advance in life if you have deep gratitude. Mistakes come from acting hastily, from acting in fear or doubt, or by forgetting of the right motive – which is more life to all and less life to none. You achieve this by focusing on the creative method and not the competitive one.

Do all that you can in a focused, efficient manner every day. Do this without haste, worry, or fear. Go as fast as you can, but never hurry.

Remember that as soon you begin to hurry or worry, you cease to be a creator and become a competitor. This is when you drop back into the old ways again. As you go on in the certain way, opportunities will come to you in increasing number. You will need to be very steady in your faith and purpose and you must keep in close touch with the infinite and the good in the world through reverent gratitude.

Again - whenever you find yourself hurrying, slow down, fix your attention on the mental image of the thing you want, give thanks that you are getting it, and then focus once more on taking action while maintaining a spirit of gratitude.

The exercise of GRATITUDE will never fail to strengthen your faith and renew your purpose. You are not to try and take anything from anyone else.

There is more than enough for all.

Yes, you should quit that crappy job.

How much more rested and inspired do you feel when you have uninterrupted time that is free from external obligations? How many of us continue working in jobs where we can't stand our bosses, or the company itself, or what it stands for, or how we are treated as employees? Why do you think we do that? In most cases, it is because we believe that these current options are the only ones we have or that we aren't worth more. That is not true. In other words, don't believe that you're obligated to stay in a job you hate just because you feel like it's all that is available to you. You're better than that. There is plenty of opportunity out there. It will take work, effort, trial, and error to get where you want to go but you can do it if you put your mind to it and commit to the journey and your goals.

What kinds of things do you do when you are not constantly reacting and responding to the whims and desires of an employer or other obligations? Think on this for awhile. In your answers to these questions is a key to the types of things that bring you joy. Look at each place of work as a stepping stone to help you reach your next place of work until you reach the goals that you have for yourself. At the same time, do not tolerate abusive and disrespectful behavior by your superiors just to hold down a job. It isn't worth it. Leverage your network of friends, family, and fans and ask for help finding the kinds of opportunities that you seek. People are much more willing to help than most people are to ask. You never know until you try.

What do you have to lose? Your crappy job? Your anxiety? Your self-doubt and despair? Those miserable fake-friends who do more to sabotage your goals and dreams than they do to encourage you? As I've said before and will say again: no one is going to give you permission to pursue your goals of a better life. It's got to be you who makes that choice.

If you feel like you don't know how to get started and are ready to do the work, hit me up at ScienceOfGettingRich.info for a consultation. Let's do this.

Without a humble but reasonable confidence in your own powers, you cannot be happy.

- Norman Vincent Peale -

chapter 14:
the impression
of increase

Whether you decide to change your career path or not, your actions in the present moment must be focused on the business in which you are now engaged.

You can get into the business you want by making constructive use of the business you are already working in by doing your daily work in a certain way. As much as your business consists in dealing with other people, whether in person, by written correspondence, or on the phone, the main thought of all your efforts must be to *convey to their minds the impression of increase.*

Increase is what all people are seeking. It is the urge of creativity within them seeking fuller expression. The desire for increase is inherent in all of nature. It is the fundamental impulse of the universe. All human activities are based on the desire for increase. People are seeking more food, more clothes, better shelter, more luxury, more beauty, more knowledge, more pleasure, more education, more wealth, and more health. We all seek various kinds of increase and a more expressive, complete life.

Every living thing is operating with this necessity for continuous advancement. Where the increase of life ceases, dissolution, stagnation and death set in at once. Humanity instinctively knows this, and hence we are forever seeking more. This law of perpetual increase was mentioned by Jesus in the parable of the talents. Only those who seek and gain more retain any, and "from those who have not shall be taken away even that which they have." It is an issue of first stewarding well what we have while in the pursuit of more.

The normal desire for increased wealth is not an evil or reprehensible thing. It is simply the desire and aspiration for a more abundant life.

People are attracted to those who can give them more of the means of life. In following the certain way as described in the previous pages, you are getting continuous increase for yourself and you are giving it to all with whom you deal.

You are a creative center from which increase is given off to all. Be sure of this and convey this to every person with whom you come in contact. Even if it is only a short interaction with a restaurant worker or grocery clerk, the selling of a single product in a local market, or a phone call to pay a bill – put into it the thought of abundance and increase. Show them this increase in action and in how you treat them. Convey and demonstrate the impression of advancement, gratitude, and abundance in everything you do so that all people shall receive the impression that you are an advancing person and that you advance and assist all who deal with you. This is especially important with the people whom you meet in a social way *(without any thought of business and to whom you do not try to sell anything)*. Give them the impression and thought of increase. If you treat others well, that will come back around to you. The inverse is also true. You can convey a positive impression by holding the unshakable faith that you, yourself, are on the path of increase and by letting this faith inspire, fill, and permeate your every action.

Do not boast or brag of your success or talk about it unnecessarily. True faith is never boastful.

Wherever you find a boastful or arrogant person, you find one who is secretly doubtful and afraid. Simply choose to feel faith and gratitude and let it work into every transaction. Do everything with generosity and the conviction that you are an advancing and successful person who is sharing advancement with everybody. Feel that you are getting rich, and that in so doing you are making others rich and passing those benefits on to all who you meet. Let every action, tone and look express the quiet confidence that you are getting rich and even that you are already rich. Words will not be necessary to communicate this feeling to others. They will see it in your actions. They will feel the sense of increase, abundance, generosity, and gratitude when in your presence and will be attracted to that in you.

Change the game - don't let the game change you.

*Money is not "the root of all kinds of evil." The **love** of money is. **Extreme greed is the root of all kinds of evil**. We are not talking about greed here. We are talking about creating the life you desire in a way that harms no one and brings more benefit to all. There is a big difference between arrogance and confidence. Arrogance feels the need to tell everyone about how great they are at the expense of others. Arrogance is always focused on "winning" and being "the best." Confidence is focused on playing the game for the joy of it. Confidence is seen in those who are at work building and creating while taking no thought of how they can outsmart or beat someone else. Arrogance is focused on outcomes while confidence is focused on the process and the practice. It is not about how much money you make. It is about how you made that money in the first place. If you had to resort to doing things that harmed others in your pursuit of more wealth, was it really worth it? Don't lose your soul in a joyless chase for power and profit.*

Regarding conveying the sense of increase to others, this can feel very difficult if you are in situations that feel like the polar opposite of what you would consider "rich." Remember the bit about gratitude though: when you are feeling low and frustrated, step back from your bank account, walk away from all the unpaid bills, and take stock of what you DO have. Be intentionally thankful for what you have right where you are – even if that is as simple as a roof over your head, food to eat, and the breath in your lungs. There are plenty of people around the world who struggle with even those basic needs. Being "rich," as we have discussed throughout the book so far, is only partially a financial thing. You are the one who has to decide how you define what your "rich life" looks like. Yes, being rich will often mean you have more money in the bank - but in your pursuit of that, don't neglect the perspectives that you adopt along the way or the people who helped you get where you are. Don't let the consumerism and cynicism of our age distract you from the blessings you have. As the philosopher Epicurus said, "Do not spoil what you have by desiring what you have not."

See that you give to others a use value greater than the cash value you are taking from them.

Your goal is to impress upon others that in associating with you, they will get increase, blessings, and wisdom for themselves *(and to actually do what you can to make that happen, of course).* Take an honest pride in doing this and let everybody know it with your actions and how you conduct yourself. You will have no lack of customers. People will go where they are given increase and you will become known as someone who can help solve creative problems. This will bring more people into your network, which will bring new opportunities. Your business will increase rapidly, and you will be surprised at the unexpected benefits that will come to you.

Each day that you work in an efficient manner, you will make more and better connections, secure greater advantages, and have increased opportunities to move into a more pleasant career if you desire. In doing all this, you must never lose sight of the vision of what you want and your faith and reason to get what you want. Let me here give you another word of caution in regard to motives:

Beware of the insidious temptation to seek to wield power over other people.

Nothing is so pleasant to the unformed, narcissistic, or partially developed mind as the wielding of power or dominion over others. The desire to rule for selfish gratification and greed has been the curse of the world. For countless ages, kings, conquerors, oligarchs, mafias, and lords have drenched the earth with blood in their foolish battles to extend their dominions. They have done this not to seek more life for all, but to get more power and control for themselves.

Today, many of the primary motives in the business and industrial world are the same. Selfish people marshal their armies of dollars, lawyers, and lobbyists to lay waste to the lives and hearts of millions in the same mad scramble for power over others that the conquerors of the past had in their hearts.

Commercial kings, like political kings, are often motivated by this type of lust for power and it leads to great ruin over the long term. Do not seek power for power's sake. Do not seek to lord over anyone. You would not like that for yourself.

The mind that seeks for mastery over others is the competitive mind, and the competitive mind is not the creative one.

Jesus saw in this desire for mastery over others the primary impulse of that evil world-view he sought to overthrow. He did not mince words when dealing with these types, and they hated him for it. Read the twenty-third chapter of the book of Matthew in the Bible to see how he views the desire of the Pharisees to be called "master," to sit in the high places, to domineer over others, and how he speaks of those who lay burdens on the backs of the less fortunate. Note how he contrasts this lust for dominion with the brotherly love that is found in seeking the common good. It is to this that he calls his followers.

Beware of the temptation to be praised as an authority, to be recognized publicly as a "master," to be considered as one who is above the common person, to impress others by lavish displays of power and wealth, and so on. In order to master your environment and your destiny, it is not at all necessary that you should rule over anyone. When you fall into the world's struggle for the high places, you begin to be conquered by fate and environment, and your getting rich becomes a much more difficult matter of chance and speculation instead of through intention and manifesting your creative ideas.

No better statement of the principle of creative action can be formulated than the favorite declaration of the late "Golden Rule" Jones who said: ***What I want for myself, I want for everybody.***

Beware of the competitive mindset! Instead, focus on creating and gratitude.

Greed is NOT good - and we must do better.

It doesn't take a rocket scientist to figure out that what Wattles is saying in this chapter is spot on...and he wrote these words over a hundred years ago! Those who seek wealth and power for the sake of wealth and power are on constant, high-resolution display in the media. Unless you've been living under a rock for the last few decades, you may have noticed that there is a staggering, almost unfathomable level of wealth, power, and income inequality on our planet at the moment. We've got a lot of work to do if we are going to build a more just and healthy society together. It starts here and now with your choice to do so. It starts with abandoning the hopelessness that tells you that things will never be better and by choosing to DO better.

I believe this chapter is one of the most important in the entire book if you are seeking to grow and advance personally, professionally, and financially... but only if you want to do so in a way that doesn't leave you feeling empty, miserable, and full of regret. On this journey of life that we share, adopting the "golden rule" is something that pretty much everyone from every religion or political affiliation can (or at least should!) agree upon. If they don't see things that way, they probably shouldn't be in a position of power. They likely are operating from the competitive mind which only creates problems and conflict. History shows proof of this concept if you think about what tends to happen when those in positions of authority use their power to manipulate, control, or domineer over others. It's never pretty in retrospect. Treat others the way you want to be treated. Choose to do and be better.

We can and must break these unhealthy societal and cultural patterns. Focus on your actions in your sphere of influence and make sure that you aren't getting caught up in the fruitless pursuit of power for its own sake. It is not sustainable and the lust of that kind of power over others will not bring you joy or peace. It is a painful and crowded road full of broken dreams and the despair of those who lost what was most important to them by their choice to travel upon it. Steer clear of that path and blaze a better one.

Other people's opinions
of you do not have to
become your reality.

- Les Brown -

chapter 15:
the advancing person

No matter what you do for a living, if you can add value and abundance to the lives of others and make them aware of this fact, they will be attracted to you and you will get rich.

What I have said in the last chapter applies as much to the professional individual and the wage-earner/employee as it does to the one who is engaged in building their own business endeavors. This applies whether you are an artist, a musician, a writer, a physician, a student, a teacher, a grocery clerk, a restaurant worker, an aspiring entrepreneur, a delivery person, a pastor, or any other type of profession.

The physician who holds the vision of themselves as a great and successful healer and who works toward the complete realization of that vision with faith and purpose as described in former chapters will come into such close touch with the source of life that they will be phenomenally successful. Patients will come to them in throngs. There are great opportunities for practitioners of the healing arts to carry out the teaching of this book. It does not matter to which of the various schools you may belong, for the principle and goal of healing is common to all of them and may be reached by all alike. The advancing person in medicine who holds to a clear mental image of themselves as successful and who obeys the laws of faith, purpose, empathy, and gratitude will see great success.

In the field of religion and faith, the world cries out for leaders who can teach their hearers the true science of an abundant life. This is the "gospel" that the world needs...not more of the old ways of hellfire, fear, guilt, shame, condemnation, and brimstone. Truly good news will give the increase of life. People will hear it gladly, and they will give abundant support to the person who brings it to them.

What is now needed are demonstrations of the science of life and abundance where they can be found. People must be shown how to succeed.

We want preachers and leaders who can not only tell us how, but who in their own lives will show us how. We need preachers and leaders who will be rich, healthy, great, and beloved, to teach us how to attain these things. Those who do will find a numerous and loyal following. The same is true of the teacher who can inspire their students with the faith and purpose of a better, ever-advancing life. They will never have trouble finding work or students to teach. Any teacher who has this faith and purpose can give it to their pupils. They cannot help giving it to them if it is part of their own life and practice.

Getting rich is an exact science. What is true of the teachers, leaders, preachers, and physicians mentioned above is true of the lawyer, the dentist, the real estate and insurance agents, the grocery clerks and the artist. This is true of everybody. The combined mental and personal action I have described is infallible; it cannot fail. Every person who follows these instructions steadily, perseveringly, and to the letter, will get rich. The law of the increase of life is as mathematically certain in its operation as the law of gravitation.

Some disclaimers, cautions & clarity

Again, I can make no direct promises as to how much "richer" you will get as you read and apply the principles in this book to your daily life since "getting rich" is always going to be a subjective term depending on your perspective. However, I will say that since applying a number of the principles presented here to my own life, I have seen tangible results, increased earnings, influence, connections, and more opportunities. The fact that you're reading this right now is proof of this concept. Take that for what it's worth. I will not so dogmatically say that this is the only way to do something or "this is an exact science" as Wattles says several times in the book. I mention this repeatedly so you can't ever say I said otherwise :)

If for some reason it's not been abundantly clear: **I am not a medical doctor or a certified financial advisor.** *While I agree with a number of Wattles' principles on a variety of topics, nothing in this book is to be considered medical, technical, or detailed financial advice of any kind. As always, consult a professional if you have specific medical or financial concerns. (And no, those sketchy videos and memes on Aunt Karen's social media pages still don't count as professional advice.)*

Don't get stuck thinking this is all "just some prosperity gospel nonsense." *As I've mentioned earlier, chances are pretty high if you're reading this book that you have at least some experience (good and bad) in spiritual or faith-based environments. Even if that is not the case, it is worth noting that the word "gospel" originally meant "very good news." It is evident to most people these days that a lot of what is heard in many churches is not exactly "good news." Perhaps a useful question to ask ourselves is, "Good for who, exactly?" You'll never hear me say that faith leaders should be living some over-the-top excessive rock-star lifestyle as many do these days. Don't confuse "being rich" with "being greedy and flashy." What Wattles is saying in this chapter is that the world needs something more than getting beaten over the head with condemnation about how terrible and sinful they are every Sunday. They don't need to be told that God is going to torture them in a fiery volcano forever if they don't pray a prayer a certain way, go to a particular church three times a week, only read one version of a religious text that is thousands of years old, or forget to say five Hail Mary's before bed.*

What the world truly needs right now are tangible acts of love, life, grace, forgiveness, generosity, abundance, and the power to make a positive difference here and now...not just the unprovable promise of a better life after this one. *Regardless of what faith you adhere to (or if you don't adhere to any at all), consider that it is good news indeed to know that anyone can learn the art and science of building a better life for themselves and their loved ones. It starts with recognizing that we're all in this together and your choice to DO and BE better today than you were yesterday. You sustain all of this through daily practice, gratitude, and focused, intentional effort.*

Form a clear mental vision of what you want, and begin to act with faith and purpose.

The wage-earner and employee will find this is as effective for them as of any of the others mentioned. Do not feel that you have no chance to get rich because you are working where there is no visible opportunity for advancement or where wages are small and the cost of living is high. Do all the work you can do every day, and do each piece of work in a focused and efficient manner. Connect intentionally with the people who believe in you. Choose to learn all you can. Put the power of success and the intention to get rich and grow as a person into everything that you do.

Do not do this merely with the idea of gaining favor with your employer in the hope that those above you will see your good work and advance you. It is not likely that they will do so. The person who is satisfied with being merely a "good, obedient employee" is very valuable to their employer. It is not to the employer's interest to promote that person. To the average employer, that employee is worth more where they are. To advance in life towards the achievement of your goals, something more is necessary than to just outgrow your current place.

The person who is certain to advance is the one who has grown personally and professionally beyond their current place and who has a clear concept of who they want to be.

This person knows they can become who they want to be and is determined to BE what they want to be. Do not try to more than fill your present place with the intention or hope of simply pleasing your employer. Do so with the idea of advancing yourself and the future of your dreams and goals. Do this with a spirit of gratitude for the stepping stone that is your current place and all you have learned about yourself while you have been there. Hold the faith and purpose of increase during work hours, after work hours, and before work hours. Hold it in such a way that every person who comes in contact with you – whether family, fellow employee, or social acquaintance – will feel the power of purpose radiating from you. In this way, everyone will get the sense of advancement and increase from you. People will be attracted to you and if there is no possibility for advancement in your present job, you will very soon see an opportunity to take another job.

There is a power which never fails to present opportunity to the advancing person who is moving in obedience to universal laws. The world opens itself to you if you act in a certain way. There is nothing in your circumstances or in the current industrial or economic situations that can keep you down. If you cannot get rich working for a corporation, you can get rich in other ways. If you begin to think, act, and build in the certain creative way, you can escape from the clutches of working for the giant corporations and get on to whatever else you wish to be doing.

If a few thousand employees would enter upon the creative and certain way, the monopolies and giant corporations would soon be in a bad plight. They would have to give their employees more opportunity or go out of business.

Nobody has to work for less than what they are worth. You do not have to accept less than a living wage for the work that you do. Companies can keep people in so-called hopeless conditions only as long as there are people who are too ignorant to know the science of getting rich or are too unwilling to practice it and do something about improving their situation. Begin this way of thinking and acting and your faith and purpose will make you quick to see opportunities to better your condition. Such opportunities will speedily come and you should act and prepare to receive them accordingly, as we have discussed elsewhere.

Do not wait for a perfect opportunity to be all that you want to be. It will take time and practice to get there.

Be patient and keep creating and learning. When an opportunity to be and do more than you are now is presented and you feel impelled toward it, take it. It will be the first step toward an even greater opportunity later. It is impossible in this universe for the person who is living the advancing creative life to lack opportunities and ideas. Your challenge is to master your skills and cultivate intentional, daily action in the direction of your goals. In this way, all things shall work together for your good. The advancing person will certainly get rich if they act and think in the certain way. Let employees everywhere study this book with great care, and enter with confidence upon the course of action it prescribes. It will not fail.

You must choose to escape the rat race.

What Wattles says in this chapter is very important if you are currently working in a job you hate and want to become financially independent through your own business or artistic endeavors. Don't think for a moment that if you suddenly start talking about how you're going to change your life, get rich, and achieve your goals that your employer, friends, family, or coworkers are going to take you seriously. Chances are much higher that they will just think you are arrogant and delusional and won't want to be around you. Even worse, some may actively try to sabotage your efforts for their own selfish, insecure reasons. Instead, keep your head down and your mouth shut. Don't talk about what you're going to do. Do your work – whatever that may be – behind the scenes. Write that book or that screenplay. Learn that instrument. Make that album. Paint that painting. Apply for that better job. Volunteer for that role. Take that course. Run for office. Believe and invest in yourself – this is an internal, life-long game.

Practice, practice, practice. *Over time, your skills will increase and opportunities will arise that will make it easier for you to transition out of your current position and into a place where you are doing more of the things that you'd like to be doing. Again, I repeat - do not boast about all the things you are doing and learning, ESPECIALLY in the workplace. It is much better to let your work speak for itself over time. Austin Kleon's book "Show Your Work" is an excellent resource that expands on this topic.*

*If you are wanting to advance to a better position in your current job, that's fine - but keep in mind that the workplace can often be a very politically charged environment where most are in the competitive state of mind, not the creative one. Rare is the workplace that places a high value on creativity and doesn't simply view "go-getters" as threats to the status quo or batteries to use and abuse until they burn out. **Those unhealthy kinds of working relationships are not sustainable for you long term - and as soon as you notice you're in one, it's time to start figuring out your exit strategy.***

If you are in a situation where you are being treated poorly by your employer or any other authority figure, get out of that situation as soon as possible. Your health and safety are your most valuable assets and you must protect them. No one will do this for you.

The world is full of opportunities and you do not have to tolerate being treated unfairly, with disrespect, or paid low wages. The more that employees the world over realize that their labor is what makes their employer successful just as much as the people steering the ship, the sooner things will start changing across society for the better. You are capable of far more than you might currently believe. Apply yourself to learning new skills every day and bettering your existing skills and you will soon begin to come across new opportunities that will be stepping stones to even bigger, better ones.

Take it one step at a time, and choose to enjoy the ride. *Try not to think of "success" as something where you "get rich quick." It is more like a journey that you are on. It's not about arriving at some specific destination. It's about using what you've got where you are while you learn how to advance. I find much more peace when I'm creating and functioning from a position of rest, gratitude, and contentment instead of constantly striving for more or better things just for the sake of getting more and better things.*

*Lastly, as it pertains to the "advancing person," think about it this way: In general, people want to be around others that they perceive are "going somewhere." This is why most people who have the outward appearance of "success" amass large numbers of followers around them. This is not to say that financial success is the only type of success. It is to draw your attention to the fact that overall, if you give off the appearance (and of course, demonstrate) that you are "going somewhere" with your life, naturally people and opportunity will gravitate more towards you. **Start building.***

Great things are not
done by impulse, but by
a series of small things
brought together.

- Vincent van Gogh -

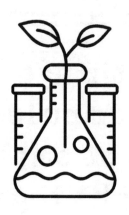

chapter 16:
cautions & concluding
observations

Many will scoff at the idea that there is an exact science of getting rich. They believe the supply of wealth is limited and will insist that social and government institutions must all be changed before any considerable number of people can acquire true wealth for themselves.

That is not true.

While it is currently the case that many existing governments keep the masses in poverty, this is because the masses do not currently think and act in a certain way. If the masses begin to move forward as suggested in this book, neither governments nor industrial systems could stop them. If the people have the advancing mind, the faith that they can become rich, and take action with the fixed purpose to become rich by the creative method, nothing can keep them in poverty. Individuals may enter upon the certain way at any time under any government and make themselves rich. When any considerable number of individuals do so under any government, they will cause the system to be modified in a way that opens the way for others.

All systems eventually must be upgraded and modified to accommodate the forward progress of a changing society. The economic liberation of the masses can only be accomplished by getting a large number of people to practice the creative and scientific method set down in this book to become rich. These will show others the way. They will inspire others with a desire for a more fulfilling and abundant life with the faith that it can be attained and a reason to pursue it.

When more people get rich with the competitive method, the worse it is for others. On the other hand, when more people get rich with the creative method, the better it is for others.

For the present, it is enough to know that neither the government under which you live nor any corrupt monopoly or capitalistic and competitive system of industry can keep you from getting rich. When you enter upon the creative plane of thought, you rise above all these things and become a citizen of another kingdom. Remember that your thoughts and focus must be kept upon the creative plane. You are never for an instant to be betrayed into thinking the supply is limited or into acting on the level of competition.

Whenever you do fall into old ways of thought, correct yourself instantly. When you are in the competitive mind, you have lost connection with the mind of the infinite. Do not waste any time in worrying how you will meet possible emergencies in the future, except as those things may affect your actions today. You should only be concerned with doing today's work in a focused, successful and efficient manner. Do not pollute your mind with worrying about emergencies which may arise tomorrow. You can attend to them as they come. Prepare and take action as necessary, yes, but do not worry or fall into the competitive mind.

Do not concern yourself with questions and fears as to how you shall surmount problems which may seem to loom upon the horizon unless you can see plainly that you must do something today in order to avoid them. No matter how tremendous an obstacle may appear at a distance, you will often find that if you go forward in the certain way, the obstacle will disappear as you approach it or you will find a way over, through, or around it. No possible combination of circumstances can defeat a person who has set out to get rich along strictly scientific and creative methods. No person who does this can fail to get rich any more than one can multiply two by two and fail to get four.

Give no anxious thought to possible disasters, obstacles, panic, or unfavorable combinations of circumstances. There is time enough to meet these things if and when they present themselves in the immediate moment, and you will find that every difficulty carries within it the methods and strength for its overcoming.

Guard your speech. Never speak of yourself, your affairs, or of anything else in a discouraged or discouraging way.

Never admit the possibility of failure, or speak in a way that infers failure as a possibility. Never speak of the times as being hard, or of business conditions as being doubtful. Times may be hard and business doubtful for those who are on the competitive plane, but they can never be so for you.

You can create what you want, and you are above fear. When others are having hard times and poor business, you will often find your greatest opportunities because you have trained yourself to see them and act despite circumstances. Train yourself to think of and to look at the world as if it is something which is becoming, which is growing; and to regard seeming evil as being only that which is undeveloped and passing away. Always speak in terms of advancement. To do otherwise is to deny your faith and to deny your faith is to lose it.

Never allow yourself to stay stuck feeling disappointed. You may expect to have a certain thing at a certain time and not get it at that time and this will appear to you like failure. If you hold to your faith and keep moving forward, you will find that the failure was only apparent. Go on in the certain way, and if you do not receive that thing, you will receive something so much better that you will see the seeming failure was really a great success. A student of this science had set his mind on making a certain business deal which seemed to him at the time to be very desirable, and he worked for some weeks to bring it about. When the crucial time came, the thing failed in a perfectly inexplicable way. It was as if some unseen influence had been working secretly against him. He was not disappointed. On the contrary, he chose to focus on gratitude and went steadily on with a grateful mind. Soon after, a much better opportunity came his way that he would not have made if he had taken the first deal. He saw that something which knew more than he knew had prevented him from losing the greater good by entangling himself with the lesser.

That is the way every apparent failure will work out for you if you keep your faith, hold to your purpose, have gratitude, and do every day all that can be done that day, doing each separate act in a successful and efficient manner. When you make a failure, it is because you have not asked for enough or have not adequately prepared to receive what you seek. Try again. Keep going until you succeed.

Keep moving forward in an efficient, grateful, and focused manner.

If you do this, you will not fail because you lack the necessary talent to do what you wish to do. If you go on as I have directed, you will develop all the talent that is necessary to achieve your goals. It is not within the scope of this book to deal with the science of cultivating talent, but it is as certain and simple as the process of getting rich.

Do not hesitate or waver in fear that you will fail for lack of ability when you come to any particular point in your journey. Learn and practice daily.

You will develop the right skills over time and the ability will be there for you. The same source of ability which enabled the untaught Abraham Lincoln to do the greatest work in government ever accomplished by a single man is open to you. You may draw upon the infinite intelligence that is there for wisdom to use in meeting the responsibilities which are laid upon you. Go forward in full faith.

Study this book. Make it your constant companion until you have mastered all the ideas contained in it. Especially as you are getting firmly established in this, you will do well to stay away from places where conflicting ideas are shared in lectures, sermons, or in media. Surround yourself with people who support you in your goals – not those who create doubts and fears within you.

Do not read pessimistic or conflicting literature or get into pointless and unfruitful arguments about the matter. Spend most of your leisure time in contemplating and taking action upon your vision, cultivating gratitude, and in reading this book. It contains all you need to know of the science of getting rich. You will find all the essentials summed up in the following chapter.

As you think, so you shall be.

Staying positive can feel like a very difficult thing to do given the nature of the noise and chaos of mass-media these days. It can seem like everywhere we look, there is drama, violence, fear, war, corruption, and that the whole world is falling apart. This is not true. Statistically speaking, people around the world are living longer, healthier, and are better educated than ever before in human history. You would not know this if you get most of your information from the corporate news media on the right OR the left of the political aisle. As I've said before and will say again: it doesn't have to be this way. That kind of fear-based culture is not sustainable or healthy for anyone. It is not the type of world-view that is worth spreading or continuing to adhere to if you want to see things change for the better. We can and must do our part to create a better future for the next generation.

Use your creative energy as a force for good. *The money will come. Focus your attention on what you can do, what you can create, and who you can connect or collaborate with right where you are. Don't waste your precious energy and time in fear and raging about things beyond your control. Those who spread such negativity are profiting from division and distraction at your expense in order to maintain power for themselves. How does that make you feel? (If the answer is "not good," then congratulations, you have a soul!)*

The best course of action is to protect your attention and use it to create and connect with like-minded people. *If you are passionate about making a positive difference in the world, good! Get involved in your local community. Volunteer to help out at a non-profit. Run for office. Create art that inspires those who see it. Be intentional about meeting people who grew up in different cultures or countries than you did. Stay out of the competitive mindset!*

Choose to invest in your own personal growth, health, and wealth. *Build something that you can look back and be proud of. You can do it. Yes, really.*

No one ever said this was easy – but I promise you that the journey and the payoff for the work required is worth it.

Your perception will define your reality. There have been many periods of extreme hardship and feelings of soul-crushing disappointment thus far in the course of my career as an entrepreneur, an artist, and an author. Choosing to handle "failure" with an attitude of resilience and the drive to get better next time is certain to help you grow as a person. I know it has done so for me. Learn from your mistakes. Don't get stuck in them. I have so many questions about the nature of our universe and the way the world works, but if there's one thing I know for sure, it's that it does not serve me or anyone to remain in a depressed, fearful mindset. What you feed your mind and the perspective you choose to take on things will define the way you view the world around you and the actions you take next. Choose wisely.

Differentiating between what I can change and what I can't change is always certain to help me refocus my efforts in a positive direction. As far as I can tell, that is "the certain way" that Wattles refers to again and again in this book. I've wasted countless hours of my life looking behind me in regret about dumb, ignorant, or hurtful things I've said, done (or didn't do), fretting about the future, or complaining about my perceived lack of opportunities. It simply is not useful to do so. Snapping out of this bad habit of mental swamp-diving takes practice, time, and effort – but life is a lot better when you actively work on staying mindful, present, and grateful. You must choose to cultivate the daily discipline to build a more abundant, creative, and joyful life. Again – this is a choice, not a feeling.

Things will only start changing for you when you shift your focus from what you don't have to what you do have and pay more attention to what you can do right here and right now. If it's something you can't control, change your focus and take action. Make sure to check out the resources in the back of this book for a decision map that I use to help myself get unstuck.

Talent is developed and practiced rigorously over time. It might seem like some people are just born with extreme talent, but a curious thing appears when you study the behavior of those individuals: they all practice their craft with focused intention and spend almost obsessive amounts of time getting better at what they do. Those who are "rich" and "successful" are usually the people who devote a lot more time and energy working on bringing their dreams and ideas to life than the average person who is working some job they hate just to pay the bills. That's not something that you may want to hear if you are looking for a shortcut – but it is the truth.

The development of talent and riches all boils down to a few things: focus, self-discipline, work, practice, and learning to roll with the punches of life instead of letting them keep you down.

Success is a journey, not a destination. *If you know this going into any endeavor, it becomes much easier to deal with the inevitable setbacks that you will encounter along the way. Remember why you got started in the first place and stay the course. Give yourself the time, grace, and patience to develop an attitude of restful, curious, and playful creative expression. Creativity should feel more like you're playing a game that you enjoy, not like an obligation or some kind of stressful work. Don't push yourself so hard that you burn out. You will be healthier and happier if you set aside time to rest and play. For more on this, read "Play" by Stuart Brown and Christopher Vaughan and "Rest" by Alex Soojung-Kim Pang. Chances are high that you would regret wasting your life if it just consists of staying zoned out in front of a screen, frittering your time away watching TV shows or mindlessly browsing social media and the internet as a form of escapism.*

Decide to create a life that you don't want to escape from. *You have the power within you to accomplish this, but it's on you to make that decision. The question is...what are you going to DO about it? Go get it, champ.*

Our deepest fear is not that we are inadequate - it is that we are powerful beyond measure.

It is our light, not our darkness that most frightens us. Your playing small does not serve the world.

We ask ourselves, "Who am I to be brilliant, gorgeous, talented, and fabulous?" Actually, who are you not to be? You are a child of God.

There is nothing enlightened about shrinking so that other people won't feel insecure around you. We were born to make manifest the glory of God that is within us - and it is not just in some of us. It is in everyone.

As we let our own light shine, we unconsciously give other people permission to do the same. As we are liberated from our own fear, our presence automatically liberates others.

- Marianne Williamson -

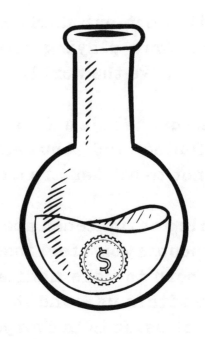

chapter 17:
a summary of the
science of getting rich

- **There is a thinking stuff from which all things are made.** In its original state, this force permeates, penetrates, and fills the empty spaces of the universe.

- **A thought in this substance produces the thing that is imagined by the thought.**

- **Humanity can form things in their thoughts.** By impressing their thoughts and imagination upon formless substances *(paper, clay, musical scales, white boards...any kind of blank canvas)*, people can cause the things they think about to be created.

- **In order to do this, humanity must pass from the competitive to the creative mind.** Otherwise, they cannot be in harmony with the spirit of the formless intelligence, which is always creative and never competitive in spirit.

- **Humanity may come into full harmony with the formless substance by entertaining a lively and sincere gratitude for the blessings in their lives.** Gratitude unifies the mind of humanity with the intelligence of the formless substance and brings about peace, perspective, and mental clarity.

- **Humanity can remain upon the creative plane only by uniting themselves with the formless intelligence through a deep and continuous feeling of gratitude.**

- **You must form a clear mental picture of what you want.** Do all that can be done every day with focus, faith and purpose to achieve your goal, doing each separate thing efficiently and without distractions.

- **You must keep the mental vision of your goals in your thoughts while being deeply grateful that your desires are being granted to you.** The person who wishes to get rich must spend their leisure hours in contemplating their vision and taking action in earnest thanksgiving that their goals are being realized.

- **It is of vital importance to frequently meditate on your vision and to join that with unwavering faith, action, and devout gratitude.** This is the process by which the creative forces are set in motion.

- **You must act NOW upon the people and with the things in your present environment.** The creative energy works through the established channels of natural growth and through the industrial and social order. What you want will come to you through the ways of established trade and commerce.

- **In order to receive your own when it comes, you must be active and this activity must consist in the pursuit of growth and more than filling your present place.** You must keep in mind the purpose to get rich through the realization of your mental image/vision.

- **You must give to everyone a use value that is greater than the cash value you receive, so that each transaction creates more life and benefits those you work with.** You must so hold the advancing mindset that the impression of increase will be communicated to all with whom you come in contact.

Those who practice these instructions will certainly get rich.

The riches they receive will be in exact proportion to the definiteness of their vision, the clarity of their purpose, the steadiness of their faith, their attention to taking practical, creative action, and the depth of their gratitude.

Learn to sell & learn to build. If you can do both, you will be unstoppable.

Earn with your mind, not with your time.

- Naval Ravikant -

final thoughts & reflections
afterword by Ryan J. Rhoades

This is not the end. It's the beginning of a brand new creative adventure. Let's wrap up with some thoughts on how we got here, where to go next, and guideposts for the path ahead.

As you and I wind down our time together and as I finish up this new edition of the book, I wanted to share some more about the journey so far as well as a peek behind-the-scenes of what went into getting the book into your hands. Writing and publishing this edition was a much more intense process than I thought it would be. It wasn't long before I found myself wrestling with the content all over again and realizing how many ways in which I needed to hear and apply the principles within it once more. So much has changed in our world since I self-published the first edition in 2018. Heck, there's been a lot of crazy stuff that has happened even since I started working on this edition in June of 2020. I wouldn't have felt right about publishing the book without addressing some of those things and how I have worked through the challenges of the moment.

I'm writing this in May of 2021 and the COVID-19 pandemic has ravaged the planet and disrupted life as we all knew it. My home state of Oregon was devastated by horrendous wildfires and I couldn't go outside for over a week because of the thick ash and smoke in the air. The sky was red for days. Then we had ice storms that knocked power out in my city for a week. There was also a violent insurrection attempt at the US Capitol...*and* at the Oregon State Capitol, which is not all that far from my apartment. There is even more division and confusion about what's real and what isn't than there was just a year ago. A lot of people around the world are dealing with levels of uncertainty and fear about their lives, their finances, and their well-being more than ever before. I count myself among those people.

We're all doing a lot of soul-searching and asking ourselves hard questions about how we want to be spending our time and what we want to be doing with our energy and attention. We're all asking questions about what really matters in life.

We are wrestling with our own mortality, existential dread, beliefs and leaders that have failed us, and what it means to live a life of meaning and purpose. Basically, we all are trying to figure out what the heck we should do about the collective messes we're swimming around in. Pretty much everyone is feeling overwhelmed, burnt out, and exhausted. Hey, that's at least something we can all agree on, right? As challenging as all of this has been, I do consider the fact that so many people are asking those kinds of deeper questions at least one silver lining from all the insanity we've been dealing with.

You can always find silver linings if you choose to look for them, but there are even more if you choose to *create* them in the midst of the chaos. You have chosen to do that by finishing this book, and that gives me hope. You have now begun a whole new adventure of creative discovery. I'm so excited for you! Whatever you do, don't let the tragedies of our times rob you of the joy and growth that you can choose to develop despite the things you see happening elsewhere or on a screen.

First and foremost, I want to express my heartfelt thanks and kudos to you for reading this and the time you've chosen to invest in yourself and your community by sticking through to the end. Things sure do feel crazy out there and it takes a special kind of grit and perseverance to get through any book – let alone one that is going to challenge you to think differently about your beliefs, your decisions, your wealth, and your future in the midst of numerous colliding and compounding global crises. No pressure, right? I'm sure that all these problems we're dealing with has something to do with all of us entitled millennials and our avocado toast, but we can talk about that another time.

We have covered a lot of ground and poked at a lot of mindsets that probably brought things to the surface for you to think about. This book certainly has done so for me each time I've read it, and even more so each time I have published new versions of it or shared its principles with friends. As you continue to pursue your art, your creativity, and your future success by applying the concepts you have learned, don't lose sight of the fact that each step in the journey is important even if it doesn't feel like it at the time.

You never know where a step you take today might lead tomorrow.

As I write these words, I'm facing a publishing deadline in a few days...and I feel terrified.

I've never had my work published by a "real publisher" before – and I can feel my heart pounding in my chest and my hands starting to sweat at the mere thought of it. I've struggled to finish this book more than any project I've worked on in almost 25 years of doing "creative work." The idea of the work being seen by a wider audience and helping more people around the world is both exhilarating and terrifying. The planet feels like a much scarier place in 2021 than any time I can think of...but with that fear also comes a kind of curiosity. It makes me wonder about where the fear comes from and why any of us ever listen to it in the first place. It makes me poke and prod at those nagging anxieties until I can take them apart, see them for what they really are, and make the choice once more to do the work of overcoming them. We all have that noise in our heads about how we aren't good enough or that we're just going to be exposed as frauds, or that things will never change for the better. That fear is always going to be there at some level. Your job going forward is to kick it out of the driver's seat of your life and find a reason to keep going regardless of what it screams at you from the back seat.

What keeps me going despite the fear is hope. I have hope because I know if you're reading this right now, you've already made the decision to stay curious and pursue a better life for yourself. If you've made it this far, you've already made the choice that you're going to figure out whatever it is that you're trying to figure out. You wouldn't have kept reading if you were just going to give up. Put another way: you didn't come this far just to come this far. So yes, you've got to keep going. It's a choice, every moment of every day. You must be the one to define what success looks like for you. You must define what is most important to you and create meaning for yourself and your life. This is a life-long process.

Viktor Frankl said, "When we are no longer able to change a situation, we are challenged to change ourselves."

I have hope because you have made that choice. I know for certain that creativity can heal at least some of the broken things in our world. I can say that because it has healed me in ways that I don't think I'll ever fully understand. Reading this book will have you forever thinking much more about your art, what you're capable of, and how you can go about bringing your ideas to life.

Knowing that you are intentionally cultivating your creativity and working towards building a better life for yourself brings with it a whole roller-coaster of emotions for me. There is a lot of division in my country right now and it can sometimes feel like everything is just a powder keg waiting to explode. The fact that you're reading something like this *despite all of that* means that you've already chosen a different path than more of the same senseless wars, drama, and petty power and status games that our species has engaged in for far too long. We may not know each other personally, and we may not agree on matters of politics, religion, or the logistics of how we should approach solving our collective challenges. We may come from different cultures, or races, or have different preferences about a whole host of things. However, if you are worried about how to pay your bills, take care of your family, and solve some kind of financial or health challenge, we are on the same path. I know how you feel right now and I would consider you a friend and an ally in those struggles. What I have written so far and the remainder of what I share here is the same advice that I would give to my closest friends and loved ones. It is the same advice I need to hear and heed myself.

Know this: the challenges you face are not permanent. You're not alone, and you can overcome the crap that life throws at you.

It will take time, effort, discipline, and a whole lot of trial and error...but I promise you that the rewards of developing your creative, business, and relationship skills are well worth the work that is necessary to do so. It makes life worth living. When you're so used to the grind of always looking for that next paycheck and waking up every day worried about how you're going to make ends meet, you eventually get used to functioning like that. Somewhere along the line, you start to think that your present reality will be exactly like your future. If you stay stuck there long enough, you end up believing the noise in your head that tells you it's always going to be this way and that none of the things you're building or trying to build will ever really go anywhere. You start to feel like you should just give up now and that you can't go on.

You start to wonder if anyone really cares at all or if anyone will ever reward or recognize you for the blood, sweat, and tears you've put into whatever it is that you're doing. Then you'll start questioning your self-worth and look for external validation and happiness from some outside source or how much money you have in the bank.

Finally, if you stay *there* long enough, you start questioning whether your life even matters at all, and that sucks. A lot. I know because I've been there. *A lot.* So listen, my friend – if you get nothing else from this book and if no one has ever told you, please hear what I'm about to say to you:

Your life matters. You are unique and deserving of love – and you can get out of the hole that you're in. The greatest form of wealth is found in loving yourself. I'm glad that you are here, and you are here for a reason.

I'll say part of that again in case you glanced over it.

The greatest form of wealth is found when you truly love yourself. If that statement made you cringe, roll your eyes, feel strange or laugh, take a few moments and ask yourself why you think that is. Loving yourself means having the courage to recognize when where you are isn't where you want to be. It means being willing to face your fears and your pain and your trauma and your depression and your anxiety. It means acknowledging to yourself that the situations you're avoiding aren't going to get any better by avoiding them. As Marcus Aurelius said centuries ago, "the obstacle is the way." The question isn't whether you know what the problems are. You do. The question is and will continue to be: **what are you going to do about them?**

Loving yourself means taking a long, hard look in the mirror and inquiring why you have such a hard time respecting the person looking back at you. You need to choose to start giving yourself more credit. You must choose to be grateful for how much you've accomplished so far and all that you've overcome. You must choose to put the spotlight of your attention on the things that make you feel alive and excited and turn away from all those fears that steal from your present and sabotage your future. You must choose to work at changing your perspective. Up to this point, you have made it through every painful moment, every traumatic event, and *everything you thought would be* a catastrophic failure or the end.

What makes you think that what you are facing now is any different than what you've overcome before?

Choose to give grace to *yourself* for how strong you are. You might not *feel strong* right now. You might not *feel like* you can beat the odds that you're up against. But you can. Financial struggles and depression often go hand in hand, and neither of them are anything to joke about. This world can be really brutal sometimes. All of us have lost friends and family to tragedy or suicide. I promise you if that is something you're considering, it is not the answer to your problems that you might think it is. The wake of destruction, trauma, grief, and pain that it leaves behind is unlike anything else. You might not think that anyone cares about you or what you're struggling with right now, but I can assure you that you're mistaken about that. I don't say so lightly and it might not feel that way, and you might not be able to see it right now, but it is the truth. Even if you think no one cares, I do.

Listen: if for any reason you feel like you are at the end of your rope and are worried that you might hurt yourself or someone else in any way, please don't. It isn't worth it. Get the help you need. Really. Doing so requires extraordinary strength. If any of what I'm saying is resonating with you right now, dig deep and imagine for a moment what your life would be like without all of the pain and the fear and the guilt and the regret and the trauma clouding your vision and weighing you down. Yes, it is possible. Yes, even for you. Yes, even for that thing that just popped in your head. It's lying to you. Defy it.

There is absolutely no shame in seeking help in any form when you realize that you need it. Doing so is a sign of strength and growth.

It is not cowardly to admit that you're not okay right now. Most of us aren't. It takes incredible strength to admit that and to be able to talk about it freely. These kinds of conversations tend to make a lot of people uncomfortable for a variety of reasons, but usually it's because they haven't done the deep work of staring into the abyss of the pain that they are carrying around and asking hard questions about how to let it go and move forward.

It's easier to stay stuck in our stuff. It doesn't require any effort whatsoever and is what we're used to. "Stuck" is our comfort zone. Growth and strength only come from doing something different and challenging. Yes, it can feel hopeless. Yes, it can feel impossible. And yes, it will sometimes feel like you'll never get out of that hole that seems to keep getting dirt piled in on you any time you make a little bit of progress. It can often feel like nothing will ever get better.

If that's how you are feeling right now, know that if I could, I would look you square in the eyes and tell you this: **I believe in you.** You are stronger than you currently feel. You have to CHOOSE to *get better* before you will *feel better*. You have to CHOOSE to *be better* before you'll ever *see something better* manifest in your life. There are so many places and people who have devoted their careers to helping people just like you. Don't rob yourself of the joys that come from connecting with them and healing from whatever challenges you have endured.

I promise you, it's worth it. There are additional resources at the back of the book if you are ready to reach out for help if you need it. Use them. I put them there for a reason. You can do this. If I can get better *(and I have)* after some of the crazy tragedies and challenges that I've experienced, so can you. Yes, really.

The thing is, when you get your identity and self-worth from other people's opinions of you or arbitrary human inventions like your job, how much money you have, "success," political parties, religious groups, profit margins and shares of stock – *of course your life will feel like it's collapsing when those things fail you.* That is why I am so adamant about this and the principles I have shared repeatedly throughout this book. I wish that I had understood these things decades ago. It would have saved me from so much heartache and unnecessary despair.

As I've said, I deeply understand what it's like to not know how I'm going to pay the next rent or grocery bill because that's exactly where I was when I first read this book. I had been living like that for a long time. I've had to accept gracious support from friends and loved ones just to pay for food or my phone bill. I've had more sleepless nights than I can count worrying about how things would work out. I've even injured myself different times from shouting into a pillow in frustration and despair. I wish I had known sooner that there's no way I can ever know how everything will work out. It is a pointless quest to try and control things that are beyond my control. I know that type of depression and paralyzing fear because it *was* my life for years.

I eventually got to a point where I was so fed up with making excuses that I no longer cared how long it was going to take or how I was going to do it. It was no longer negotiable. I was fed up with being fed up. I had made the choice that I was going to get better, no matter the cost.

You can, too.

I thought what I needed was money. What I really needed was to first change how I defined success.

I started reading the original version of this book for the first time in 2014. It didn't take long to realize the first thing I needed to do was stop paying attention to what I didn't have, and what I couldn't do – and instead focus on what I could do with what I already had. While the world outside and around me felt terrifying and uncertain, this old dead guy Wallace Wattles seemed to insist that there was a "certain way" of getting rich and creating a better life right where I was. I thought he sounded like a crazy person, to be honest. But I was desperate. I was broke. I was unemployed and had just moved to a new city where I didn't have any leads or clients for my business. I didn't have a clue how I was going to pay my rent. It was the first time my wife and I had a place of our own and I was more afraid than I have ever been in my life. I felt ashamed that I didn't know how I was going to provide for my family and there were many moments when I thought all hope was lost.

I realized if I was ever going to get out of the hole I was in, I had to cultivate hope within me. I had to tune out the noise and stop comparing my life to everyone else's.

I had to shift my perspective from trying to get rich quick like a gambler in a casino and instead learn how to plan for, design, and grow the life I wanted with patience and intention like a gardener. I learned how to garden. I learned how to build businesses. I learned how to play the piano and the guitar. I took courses and read everything I could get my hands on that might bring practical solutions to the challenges I was facing. I connected intentionally with other artists, authors, business leaders, aspiring entrepreneurs, coaches, and creators. I learned public speaking and podcasting and developed a daily writing habit. I started exercising every day and learning how to eat healthier. I chose to focus relentlessly on my own sphere of control and influence. I recognized how much of my life I was wasting by scrolling aimlessly on a never-ending news feed of drama, gossip, narcissism, misinformation, propaganda, and fear on the internet. I also realized how the vast majority of it was designed that way on purpose to grant profit and power to a small handful of greedy and opportunistic sociopaths *(read Ryan Holiday's book 'Trust Me, I'm Lying' for more on THAT topic).*

I had to choose to tune out that nonsense and focus on doing deep, creative, and intentional work instead of all the shallow, distracted, and mindless consumption. None of this was "easy"...but it did get easier as I began to look at all of these things like habits I was strengthening with each repetition.

Step by step and day by day, our opportunities grew. There were and still are bumps in the road, and I am not naive enough to think that there aren't more challenges ahead. Challenges and tragedy are part of life – but you have to make it a point to decide that you won't get stuck thinking they are the *only* things in life. Abundance, joy, beauty, peace, success, true happiness and wealth are things that you cultivate in your mind. They're things you develop within you long before you will experience them in the world around you. Circumstances have improved dramatically for my family and I compared to those earlier days, and I know for certain that many of the lessons I picked up from this book have made a big difference in my quality of life and the way I perceive and interact with the world around me. Perhaps that's what the whole "certain way" thing is about after all.

I am still not used to the reality that I am no longer in the dire financial situations that I was in for the better part of the last decade. *The Science of Getting Rich* helped me to pay more attention to the wealth of ideas and creativity within me and how to co-create with the allies I have met along the path. This book helped me give much less energy to the haters, the pessimists, and the limitless number of distractions and diversions that any creator will encounter along the way. My hope is that it will do the same for you and so much more.

Looking back, it has been hard to believe that I'm writing these words in a book that will be published and read around the world. I acknowledge that it is indeed a privilege and a blessing to be able to say that – but I am not special in that regard. Do not think for a moment that you cannot overcome whatever it is you are facing or end up in a better position than you currently find yourself in. You can do all of this. It is a matter of choosing to put in the work of becoming a life-long learner.

This isn't magic or luck. It's intention, action, and making the choice to do and be better today than you were yesterday. That's the secret.

It is a very strange feeling to no longer be stuck in a place of constant fear, hustle, and hyper-vigilance around my finances.

Make no mistake: I am beyond grateful to be able to say that. It still doesn't feel real and I regularly have to remind myself that it is. Even thinking about those days conjures up vivid flashbacks of many nights when I was laying awake in the dark, fighting off panic attacks and wondering how on earth I was going to make ends meet tomorrow. I am fully aware that there are many who will read this who are dealing with even more challenging circumstances than I can even imagine. My advice would remain the same for you as I have shared throughout the book. This is not to dismiss the intensity of the challenges ahead of you. I share these things because they're the only things that I know work consistently regardless of the circumstances.

It's the same advice that is often given by those who have survived and thrived despite trauma, betrayal, despair, war, genocide, torture, and the myriad of awful things one can experience as a citizen of this planet. It boils down to how you choose to look at where you currently are, the stories you tell yourself about what it all means, and what you decide to do about it.

If you really want to change your circumstances, you've got to start with changing your perspective about them and the actions you're taking daily.

These are the only things you can ultimately control. Everything else will just throw you off course into a tailspin of self-loathing and fruitless distractions. Poverty and wealth both begin as thoughts. They grow in the stories you tell yourself about what your circumstances mean and who you think you are. They are sustained by a combination of your beliefs, mindsets, and actions over time. You may not be able to completely stop the negative, fearful, and uncertain thoughts about your current situation or self-worth from flying through your head. However, you *do* get to choose if you are going to listen to them. You can counter this noise by regularly meditating on your goals and then daily taking action to bring those goals to life. This is about practice, not perfection. It's never too late to start creating a better life for yourself. Like so many other things we have talked about, doing this is a choice – not a feeling.

Know this: that condemning voice of fear in your head is lying to you & is not your friend. Defy it, my friend. Defy it, defy it, DEFY IT.

It's the voice that tells you that you'll never get out of the hole you're in or that you're destined to forever be broke and struggling. Again, it is lying to you. I don't know where that voice comes from, or what it is exactly, and I'm not sure it ever really goes away. But I do know it's lying to you. I can say that because it's the same stupid voice that had me convinced for over 20 years that I'd be broke forever...*except I'm not broke anymore.* Now it just tries to tell me that I'm going to lose everything I have gained and that if I do, there's no way I'll be able to recover. This too is a lie, and I can know that for certain because growth, recovery, and resilience after any failure or mistake is a decision that we all get to make.

You can choose to learn from your failures and mistakes or you can choose to keep returning to them. You can choose to listen to that lying voice, or you can choose to defy it. Choose wisely.

It's tricky, you see. The message it tries to put in your head may change its verbiage here and there, but the core tone and idea is always the same. It's always trying to convince you that you aren't good enough and that any moment now, everything is going to collapse around you. This paralyzes you into self-sabotage and inaction, which usually ends up giving you more of the same crappy mindsets and circumstances that got you here in the first place! You must pay more attention to the things you pay attention to and relentlessly focus on your consistent actions. One of the benefits of doing "creative work" over time is that you can learn how to overcome that negative voice if you actively choose to build and create *despite* it. Again, this is about daily practice and discipline. That voice will do all it can to get you to do *anything but* your creative work for the day. *Don't listen to it.* **Create every day.** Even if that just means scribbling "I DON'T WANT TO CREATE TODAY" in a notebook somewhere. Trust me, you'll feel better.

Growing up in the church, I was told that voice was the devil. Author Steve Pressfield says it's a force called Resistance that shows up to stop artists from connecting with the Muse, finding their voice, and making their art. Some Eastern cultures would call it Mara, sent to tempt you away from enlightenment. Every culture that I'm aware of refers to it in some way, shape or form and its pretty much never in a positive light.

I've stopped trying to figure out what it is or where it comes from. It doesn't matter. I don't care to debate about things like that anymore.

Whatever it is, it's lying to you and is trying to distract you from the creative power within. Let its presence clue you in to the fact that you're probably working on something that is worth making. *Defy it, defy it, defy it.*

Those things you're procrastinating and avoiding are usually the very things that you should work on every single day until they're done.

If you want to know how to write a book, it is very simple. You write it one word, one second, one sentence, one minute, one paragraph, one hour, one page, one chapter, and one day at a time. There is nothing glamorous about it at all. Anything worth doing is like that. It is a daily choice and a daily practice. It is not a feeling.

I don't share any of this to scare you away from creating your works of art. I share it with you to let you know that I'm just like you and what to expect on the path. We all have those fears. I don't *feel* like sitting here and finishing this manuscript. I feel like cowering in a corner and hiding. I feel like playing video games and avoiding doing the work that goes into finishing any big project or idea. I *feel* like doing something that will give some form of immediate and short term gratification instead of doing the difficult work of pushing through the voice of resistance and showing up every single day. The only *"feel like it"* here is the feeling of being fed up with letting my own stupid fears prevent me from publishing this book so I can move on to the next chapter of my life. If I can push through this noise in my head, you can too. Leaning into your creativity will force you to face your fears instead of running from them. Do it. The alternative is worse, I promise. It will be a process, and there will be times it hurts like hell, but it will be worth it.

What you think and what you do today will shape who you become and what you have tomorrow. Choose wisely.

My journey with this book and the principles within it began six years ago. Yours starts now. The first time I read *The Science of Getting Rich*, I had to reckon with a lot of unhealthy and unhelpful mentalities I had about money, how to make it, what to do with it, and the kinds of people who have it.

It made me ask myself hard questions about what I was doing with my life and why.

More than that, it helped me get to a place where I drew a line in the sand and decided I was going to be the kind of person who would do what I must to accomplish my goals and achieve financial independence through the creative method.

A series of whirlwinds ensued. There were some major and very scary health challenges in my family and with the people closest to me. We struggled deeply to find work, pay bills, and to maintain any sense of peace, joy, or hope. We fought through daily depression, pain, anxiety, uncertainty, and frequent panic attacks. We had to put one of our pets down because we couldn't afford the thousands of dollars of continued veterinary guesswork on her increasingly tragic health problems.

We would land deals that seemed promising but then turned into exhausting and expensive nightmares. We endured trauma, despair, and paralyzing fear. It seemed like nothing was working.

My life felt like it had been hit by a hurricane. I had a lot of rebuilding to do, and I wasn't sure where to start.

The person I cared the most about in the world was suffering in ways I didn't understand and we both felt lost and hopeless. It was like we were floating aimlessly through storms we were sure would never end. But eventually, like all storms, they did. We grew. We got better. We took classes on how to start and run a business. We learned that there is a big difference between knowing how to do something and knowing how to run a business selling that thing. We made the decision to get better at building systems that would help us run our business instead of letting our business and the circumstances of life run us. We actively sought out help and mentors from kind and compassionate people in our community who had devoted themselves to helping people like us. We connected with therapists, friends, and financial advisors. We surrounded ourselves with allies and cut toxic people, beliefs, and behaviors out of our lives. Eventually, we started landing better clients and bigger deals as we placed a higher value on our health, our time, our expertise, and our work. More opportunities presented themselves as we continued looking and building, but we were still really stressed out.

Eventually, I found a part-time job to supplement our business income. I knew I didn't want to keep offering design-for-hire services forever, but I had no idea how I was going to wind that down. It was my main source of income.

It was helping to keep our bills paid but I was burning the candle at both ends. I wasn't sure how long I could keep up with it all. The part-time job helped me start making that transition and still gave me time to work on some of my own projects, including the self-published edition. I released the first edition of the book with the hope that doing so would help me make enough extra cash to wind down the design work sooner. Despite not feeling "rich" at the time, I knew that the principles within it were working to keep me moving forward and I was definitely making more money by applying what I had learned.

However, things didn't work out how I thought they would and I didn't sell many copies. I didn't have the energy or focus to market and promote the book while also juggling so many other projects, clients, and the fallout from years of stress, health challenges, anxiety, and burnout. My wife and I had been doing design-for-hire work for almost a decade, and despite our best efforts to turn it into a sustainable and profitable endeavor, it just wasn't working out. More than that, we grew to hate so much of the "business side" of doing the work. Not a good combination.

We enjoyed the creative aspect of things but couldn't stand everything else that went into running a business built around selling design services. There were so many projects that we poured insane amounts of time and energy into that never went anywhere or didn't play out how we thought they would. We knew we needed a way out but didn't know how to get there, so I went back to the drawing board.

Minimize your information input to maximize your creative output. Keep your thoughts, attention, and actions focused on what you can control - not on all the things you can't.

There was a whole lot I couldn't control about the situations I was facing, but I knew that generosity and gratitude was always a good strategy that brought unexpected and fruitful results. I decided to stop trying to make money with the self-published edition and instead chose to try a bit of an experiment. I wanted to really test the principles that Wattles discussed with the marketing of the book itself. *(Kind of meta, right?)* The world felt crazy back then too, and I wanted to get the message out to as many people as I could.

I knew that the ideas in it had helped me stay focused and creative when everything else felt out of control. I was curious how others would fare with the material.

The constant dread of getting caught up in the doom-and-gloom narratives that social and corporate media perpetuates wasn't working so well for me, so I decided to really lean into practicing daily gratitude and focusing on what I *could* control. I made it a point to move my creative projects forward at least a little bit every day. I gave hundreds of copies of the book away and wrote off the printing and shipping costs as a marketing expense. I proofread the first edition of the book by live streaming myself reading it and answering questions to the few viewers I had over the course of several weeks. The live streams got better each time and with practice. I learned more about how to produce better quality videos and revised the book because of the feedback I was able to get in real time from the live stream.

Any clients we landed or connections we made as a result of these efforts were just a bonus. I started writing more and we intentionally began taking on less clients. I started The Creative Revolution Podcast and had the privilege of interviewing and befriending fascinating creators from all around the world, including one of my all-time favorite artists, Dan Piraro of Bizarro Comics. I wasn't seeing a significant increase in my income, but I was seeing a dramatic increase in my creative output by cutting back on how much information I was consuming.

In the midst of all of these exciting and interesting things though, my wife and I still struggled immensely to figure out what to do next. Money was still really tight and regardless of our best efforts, the business still wasn't making ends meet and various health challenges continued. My part time job was helping but it was also exhausting and unreliable as a source of long-term income. We had a ton of debt, no savings, and a series of expensive and traumatic family emergencies that we had to pay for with credit cards. **In many ways, it had already felt like we were treading water every day. Now it felt like we were drowning.**

You see, I have a very strong aversion to debt of any kind. This is largely due to over a decade of awful experiences with a private, for-profit student loan company that has been about as much fun to deal with as catching a 2x4 to the side of the face. The stress of all this would often send me into what felt like uncontrollable panic attacks. The mind is a powerful thing indeed – and if you don't do the work of learning to check the things you believe about yourself and your situation, those fearful thoughts can take on a life of their own and it won't be a life that you enjoy. That was certainly the case here. I got stuck more times than I can count feeling sorry for myself and wishing I had never taken out those loans in the first place. I had deferred payments during and after the financial crisis of 2008 and my original balance ballooned to almost twice what I had originally borrowed.

Student loans are a trap, my friend. Steer clear! Compound interest sucks when it's working against you. I felt like I had been hit by a train...but I couldn't change it. All I could do was to keep going back to the drawing board until I could figure out a way forward. What I could change was what I was doing and what I was focusing on. I knew the only way out was through.

You must be honest with yourself if you want to move forward. Complaining gets you nowhere.

We started our first business in 2011 and had put so much time and energy into it by this point. Surely "success" was just around the corner, right? Even though we no longer had any joy whatsoever at the prospect of building websites, designing logos, flyers, business cards, or any of the hundreds of things we made over the years, it still felt like I couldn't let it go because of how much we had invested into it so far. *(This is called the sunk-cost fallacy)*. I had no idea how to even start cutting off clients who were our only reliable source of monthly income. Sure, I could try to find a full-time gig, but the thought of running the business while also working 40+ hours a week for someone else filled me with absolute terror. I was already burned out and exhausted in ways I never had been before.

We had to be brutally honest with ourselves about where things were financially. Life wasn't going to get any better if we kept doing the same things we had been doing. We decided it was time to *at least try* to put the business on the back burner. It was one of the hardest decisions I've ever had to make, but my wife and I agreed that I would pick up a full-time job as soon as an opportunity to do so presented itself. It took me a long time to open up to this idea and in retrospect, I admit that I should have looked for something sooner. I felt like a colossal failure already because of how much of a struggle it had been...and now here I was admitting defeat – or at least what felt like defeat at the time.

Soon after we settled on this as the next best course of action, I was able to find a job that seemed like it would be a good fit for awhile. The regular paycheck helped significantly and I had a lot of autonomy in my role. My experience running a design business gave me insights into how to do the job that I otherwise would not have had. I got along well with my coworkers and we worked in a fun and always-changing environment. I was never bored. However, the job did bring with it a whole different kind of stress and exhaustion that I was not prepared for.

We were still juggling way too much at home with various health challenges and our business. Something had to give. We started telling some of our clients that we would no longer be able to work with them due to lack of time and bandwidth. They were all very understanding. My fears about that process were proven to be wrong. We were bringing in less money per month, but my stress level started decreasing a bit and I felt like I could see a light at the end of the tunnel. There were some definite challenges, but about six months in, I started finding my rhythm and feeling like things were looking up. I had connected well with my team and we had so many plans for what we were going to do and how we were going to do it. It was January of 2020 – a brand new year, and we thought we were ready for it.

We had no way of knowing that the whole world would soon turn upside down in ways we couldn't even begin to imagine.

In February of 2020, I started hearing some internet chatter about a virus that was alarming people around the world. I didn't know much about COVID-19 at the time, but the more I looked into it and how it was affecting countries in Asia and Europe, it became clear to me that it was going to be a big problem. There was a multi-tiered crisis of major proportions about to spread throughout the globe.

The political landscape in the US was divisive in ways unlike anything most people had ever experienced in their lifetimes. There was a colossal amount of misinformation down-playing the severity of the virus as well as how it was going to affect things here. Many wrote it off as no more serious than the flu, and admittedly I did too at first. Some in positions of power and influence did the same every day in the media and at press conferences. It was hard to know what or who to believe about pretty much anything. More than that, it was hard to know what to do. It would have been easy to just continue acting as if nothing was going on and that everything would be fine, but as I had experienced time and again over the years, I knew that wasn't a safe bet to make. Preparation and taking daily action to build despite the impending chaos was the only way I would be able to stay focused and not get caught up in the whirlwind that was headed our way.

I kept researching until there was nothing more I needed to know in order to take some preparative action. The pandemic was coming to America and most of us weren't even remotely ready for it.

As a country and a culture, we were simply not prepared for the compounding effects of so much trauma and tragedy. I don't just mean that in the sense of not knowing how to handle the effects of the virus itself on the body or in the population. I also mean how we as a society were going to handle so much staggering uncertainty, division, propaganda, chaos, confusion, racism, brutality, and civil unrest that hit us all at once. How were we going to weather the storms that were coming towards us...and in fact were now here?

I did the only thing I knew how to do when life throws a strong right hook: I prepared as best I could but then got to work doubling down on creativity, gratitude, and generosity.

I had done enough research about how the pandemic was affecting things elsewhere to know to start stocking up on groceries and other essentials before the lockdowns and the Great Toilet Paper Panic of 2020. I sent articles and suggestions to family, coworkers, and friends around the world based on what I thought was coming and practical suggestions for what they could do to prepare both their minds and their bodies. I connected with and tried to encourage friends who were 3D printing equipment for doctors during the PPE shortage. I continued gardening and learning 3D printing on the side.

I found respite amid centuries-old wisdom in the writings of the Stoics like Marcus Aurelius and Epictetus. I was convinced that there was no way to completely avoid the obstacles ahead, but I also knew that we could choose to get stronger and focus on what we could control in the midst of it all. I started sharing resources and reading recommendations *(like you will find at the back of this book)* that I knew would help my friends, clients, and coworkers get through the challenges that lay ahead. Then it dawned on me...I had created just such a resource a few years earlier that was just sitting on my bookshelf!

I hadn't been doing much promotion of the book or my business since taking on the full-time job. I felt powerless about so much of what was going on in the world around me, but the least I could do was share this book that I had already put in the work to publish. I wasn't certain about much, but I *was* certain that anyone who read it would start thinking more outside the box about how to perceive and approach their challenges. The mindsets and exercises in the book had helped me through some really tough times and I thought they could do the same for others.

My job had become much more stressful because of constantly needing to react to ever-changing and confusing restrictions in my state. By this point, our business felt like it was on life support due to most of our few remaining clients canceling services because of challenges they were facing due to COVID-19. It was time to really put some of the theories in the book to the test and see what would happen.

Share your work and surround yourself with people who believe in you. It pays off eventually.

Right around this time, my wife and I had a serious conversation about the state of our business. Was I going to take my own advice and the advice of those closest to me about how things were looking? Was I going to let my ego prevent me from acknowledging when something just wasn't working out? Could I take the leap and admit to myself that it was time to pivot to something new and different, even if the path ahead wasn't clear or predictable? I had to acknowledge to myself that this business was slowly killing my joy, putting a major strain on the most important relationships in my life, and draining my creative energy.

So despite the uncertainty of the pandemic, the division going on in the country, and a whole host of other things wildly outside of my control, we made the difficult decision to take our design business off the back burner and wind it down for good.

We hadn't told anyone yet and weren't sure how to go about doing so, but we knew for sure that we couldn't keep up with it anymore. It wasn't fair to us *or* to our clients. Trying to do client work and personal projects in the evenings or weekends along with the exhaustion of working a low wage, 40+ hours a week job in a high-stress, high-risk, politically charged environment...all during a global pandemic? No thanks. Not fun, and not sustainable. We decided that it would be best to focus any extra energy outside of my job on trying to get the book to a wider audience without worrying about trying to make a bunch of money with it.

I saw that I had been selling myself short by continuing on the path I was on. It was time to pivot. You too must learn the art of the pivot.

I wish I had read *The Science of Getting Rich* prior to *(or at least during)* the recession of 2008. Doing so would have made my response to that crisis much different than it was. I would have spent more time building and less time worrying.

Knowing this and the challenges so many were facing, I ordered a few hundred copies of my self-published edition to give to coworkers, the amazing people who delivered our mail, and to friends and creators I had met over the years. My hope was that in doing so, others would at least find some respite in their creativity during these crazy times and maybe come up with some innovative ideas for how they could generate solutions or income for themselves in new ways while being stuck at home or when they were off from work. I also wanted to express genuine gratitude to the people who were doing what often are thankless, frustrating, low-paying jobs. I've been there and I wanted to give them the same glimmer of hope that I felt years ago in that thrift store when I was aimlessly looking for a way out of the situation I was in.

Once the books arrived, I took a photo of them stacked up together and posted it on social media with the announcement that I would be doing some giveaways. I shared a brief summary of how the book had helped me and why I published it, along with some encouragement to keep creating and building despite the chaos of 2020. I knew that nothing in the book was a solution to "get rich quick," but I also knew I had nothing to lose by choosing to be generous with something that had helped me stay focused during the crazy times we were all enduring.

You can probably imagine my surprise when the very next day, I was offered a publishing deal with the company that released this expanded edition.

I had created a handful of cover designs for them years ago and the founder told me that he loved what I had done with the self-published edition. He said that book sales on entrepreneurship were up all over as people were stuck at home and coming face-to-face with harsh realities about their health and financial well-being. The offer shocked me, to be very forthright with you. It was completely unexpected and I wasn't even thinking about making a new edition. I had just worked up the courage to start really promoting the first edition! It took me several weeks of talking it through with mentors, friends, and others whose perspectives I trusted more than my own before I could even think about agreeing to the deal.

It stirred up all kinds of noise in my head and that nagging "impostor syndrome" that everyone who has ever attempted any creative endeavor knows all too well: *"Who do you think you are?"* Yes. Who, indeed?

It never even occurred to me that someone would want to re-release something I had self-published. In many ways, it forced me to take my own work more seriously. I deliberated back and forth over the contract and had it reviewed by trusted advisors and colleagues. They encouraged me to take the deal and said that I needed to stop listening to the nagging fears, but I still wasn't sure. As I write the last chapter in the book, I'm *still* not sure. Maybe we're never completely sure about things like that...but I *was* sure that my wife and I had to figure out what to do about winding down our design business. It was time to tell my clients that I was calling it quits.

You have to choose to quit the things that you know for sure aren't going to get any better.

You've probably figured out by now that I said yes to the book deal. As I mentioned, we had also just decided to say no to any more client work. We had already lost a number of clients because the pandemic had negatively impacted their business income, so in a strange way that set up an easier transition for us. *Everyone* was asking questions about how they could make some big changes and still make a living, so the process of closing things down was much smoother than I imagined it would be. I had removed one of the biggest stressors in my life at the time by winding down the design business, so I thought putting out the new edition would be simple and that I could get it done in a few months. I envisioned just changing some style elements, adding a bit of extra commentary, and fixing some typos.

Instead, I ended up redesigning the entire book and expanded the commentary significantly. I wrote another 40 page chapter that you're now reading. I had to request several extensions on the due date because life felt completely crazy. You see, the world does not care about your creative projects. You must care enough about whatever you're making to endure the nonsense that life can throw at you. And boy, does it try. I had to carve out whatever time I could while still working a full-time job during a pandemic to get this finished. In many cases that meant waking up at 4:45 or 5 AM to get a few hours in before starting at my 9-5. I would regularly hop on early morning Zoom calls with my brilliant friend Nathan Landis Funk on the other side of the country who was also working on a book as well as a new music album at the time. We kept each other going over video chat. The process felt like we had shipwrecked on an island and were trying to hack our way through the jungle with a dull machete in the dark. I'd have preferred a sharp machete and some torches of course, but hey – it was something.

Creative projects often take on a life of their own and will always take more time and effort to complete than you think they will. Plan accordingly. (I didn't)

It didn't take long before I was wrestling with some all-too-familiar fears and really big questions all over again. How the heck do you publish a book about "the science of getting rich" during one of the most intense and terrifying global economic downturns in human history? Who do I think I am to publish something like this? Am I just kidding myself that this could actually go anywhere? Will people think I'm just some arrogant, out of touch jerk who is trying to make a quick buck with a book like this? What will so-and-so think? If the book actually *is* successful, will people from my past show up and try to sabotage me because of something stupid that I said or did when I was afraid or angry? What am I hoping to accomplish? How on earth am I going to do this in time with everything else that is happening? On and on the questions went...and at the end of the day, I knew the truth: *these nagging questions didn't matter.* I either believed in the work I was doing or I didn't. I had signed the deal and I had to get to work.

As I started diving into the material again, I quickly realized how many things I was still doing that served more to burn me out instead of things that brought me happiness, wealth, peace, and joy. I had wound down my design business, yes... but the job I was in didn't seem like it was going to get any better. The stress there was mounting and morale was terrible as the pandemic and craziness of the last two years raged on. I kept writing and envisioning a better future as best as I knew how, while also keeping my eyes open for any new opportunities that might arise.

I had to choose to remain optimistic and present despite the crises. My wife and I found out that we qualified for assistance due to laws that had passed to help small business owners who had lost income because of the pandemic. This helped immensely to ease the hit from no longer having so much client income and I kept writing. We also started talking about how we were going to pivot our business endeavors to creating original products *(RDShop.biz)* that would generate income without us constantly needing to exchange our time for money, which I'll get into shortly. It was also around this time that my state was hit with devastating wildfires, horrible ice storms, nightly protests, and attempted insurrections at both my state's Capitol building and the one in DC. No big deal. This is fine.

It was starting to feel like we were living in some screwed up reality TV version of The Hunger Games.

I've been through some bizarre and challenging circumstances in the past when working on big creative projects, but 2020 and 2021 have been something else entirely. Regardless, I knew I had to once more focus on what I could control and what I was doing each day to move the project forward.

"Hey, the sky is red, full of ash and smoke, and your city might burn down!" Doesn't matter. Pack your important stuff, put it by the door in case you need to evacuate, and keep writing.

"Hey! Your city's power is out because of record-breaking ice storms!" Too bad. Doesn't change the task at hand. Bundle up, hunker down, and keep writing.

"Hey! Angry armed men waving Confederate flags and wielding bull whips broke into your Capitol building down the street and there are nightly protests against police brutality and racism! Civil unrest is everywhere!"

Can't control it – **KEEP WRITING.**

I started seeing the finish line ahead as the book was coming together. I imagined what it might be like to be able to quit my job and live by a warm, tropical beach somewhere away from the strange nightmare that it felt like I was living through. Whether that would happen or not, I had no idea...but I figured that I'd try to do what Wattles suggests throughout the book and regularly meditated on that *(currently formless)* idea. I even started playing ocean and beach sounds every morning when I would wake up to try and imagine what it would sound like if I actually did have the financial freedom to live on a beach somewhere. I knew that I had to envision and believe it before I would ever see it. I had to keep building and I had to start right where I was. You might think that sounds ridiculous, but so does staying broke and afraid. From a myriad of very detailed scientific testing *(i.e. from wasting WAY too much time doing so)* I knew that if I kept letting myself get distracted by all the drama in the news and the reality-TV-show insanity of the political landscape that I wouldn't ever get anything done. Well, at least nothing besides aimlessly doom-scrolling on a news feed until I gave myself a headache, heart palpitations, or a panic attack.

That is not exactly the kind of mental and emotional environment that is conducive to deep thought and creative work. I was sabotaging my own creativity by doing the exact *opposite* of what Wattles suggests in the book. I was paying way too much attention to "the way things are" and stressing out about things beyond my control instead of focusing on the creative method. I was worrying about the future and avoiding the present moment.

I needed to think up and create a better environment on purpose. That was one of the principles I learned from this book, so I put it to the test.

While I was working on this manuscript and stuck at home because of the lock-downs, I started building an indoor and outdoor garden in my small apartment and cultivating a 3D printing hobby thanks to an epic Christmas gift from my dad. I cleaned out my office and set up dedicated creative space to write and work on the book. The world outside and on the screens felt chaotic and scary, but at least I could start creating a better, healthier, and more enjoyable environment in my own home one day at a time. My wife and I got rid of a lot of old stuff that no longer brought us any kind of joy. *(Thanks, Marie Kondo!)* We donated or threw away things that reminded us of how broke we used to be. We made room for new things and saved up enough money to get a new keyboard so we both could play the piano more often. My wife hadn't played in years and it was a real joy to see her playing it again. I also started playing the guitar daily for the first time in ages. We weren't rolling in cash by any means, but at least we were no longer worrying about how we were going to pay the electric bill.

Thanks to a casual suggestion from my amazing cartoonist friend Brent Metcalf *(bipster.net)*, I set up some lattice on my very ugly back patio and planted clematis vines. It didn't take long for them to grow and bloom into beautiful flowers that gave my wife and I more privacy in our crappy apartment complex along with a gorgeous view. I bought some cheap hummingbird feeders and hung them in the windows, and soon we had hummingbirds showing up amidst the flowers right outside. I gardened and wrote at least a little bit every day and even planted an herb garden in front of my apartment complex for my neighbors to use if they wanted to. For the first time in my life, I actually started to "feel rich" as I focused on all the good things we had and tuned out the fear so I could work on the book.

This small home-grown sanctuary gave me peace in the midst of the storms that were raging everywhere else.

This included at work where we were all exhausted from trying to figure out how to navigate the still-changing COVID restrictions, mask mandates, and dealing with belligerent customers who were for some reason convinced that wearing a mask in public during a global pandemic was a bad idea. I didn't feel like I could keep going at this pace much longer, especially once some things reopened and I was no longer working from home. I was very grateful for the job when so many were unemployed, but I was completely fried. I was doing the work of several people but my hands felt tied with the "golden handcuffs" of a regular paycheck and medical benefits. I would wake up every morning to work on this book, go to work all day, then come home and collapse from exhaustion almost every night.

The stress of all of it was really weighing on my wife and I. We did what we could to try and remain optimistic and focused. I kept trying to imagine what a better life would look like and how to create it piece by piece, day by day. I chose to focus on gratitude as much as I could, knowing that we were building things that would grow in value over time. It wasn't easy, but I knew it was the only way forward.

True wealth and financial freedom comes from owning assets and building systems that work for you while you sleep...not from exchanging your time for money.

Having spent the last decade or so learning everything I could about entrepreneurship and startups *(because I had no idea what the heck I was doing when I got started)*, I knew that reaching my financial goals *outside* of the 9-5 life would never happen unless I owned assets that made money in the background. I also knew that the only way that *I could make that happen* was by utilizing the creative method and what was already at my disposal like Wattles mentions in the book. The same is true for you. Before we wrap up, let's talk a little bit about money and your mindsets about it. Whether you are in a job that you love or are struggling through one that you absolutely despise, my hope is that you have at least *started* thinking about how to create those types of assets for yourself by this point in the book.

Manifesting your ideas is one thing. Monetizing them is another. Doing so depends on your ability to recognize, believe in, and assign a value to what you have created. Assets could be things like books you'll write, investments you'll make, software you'll develop, expertise and sweat equity you've developed in certain fields, custom products you'll design, real estate you'll own, music or art that you'll create, businesses or non-profits that you'll start, and even relationships you'll develop that compound in value over time as you cultivate them. The options are limitless here and they only increase as you harness the power of your creativity over time. This is the power of the creative method over the competitive one.

To your employer, your labor, your creative energy, and your time are assets that they leverage into productivity and profit for themselves and their shareholders. They recognize the value that your energy, creativity, and the work you do brings to the company that *they* own. Your work makes them rich. **The question now becomes...*do you recognize your value?*** If not, it's time to flip the script.

Put bluntly, getting rich and achieving true financial independence as an employee in a standard 9 - 5 situation is impossible.

By definition, you are not financially independent if your main source of income depends on exchanging your time for money. The goal here is not to work *more* or to work *harder*. The goal is to work *smarter*. Ultimately, you want your money and creativity to work for you, not just for someone else. This becomes especially important when things happen to your main source of income that are beyond your control. That could be things like your company getting bought out by some soulless corporate monolith that shuts down your department and lays everyone off, or if you get sick for a long period of time and run out of paid sick days, or if a pandemic forces your boss to let you go because they have to close down the business. The situations don't really matter. You want to develop multiple streams of income for yourself just in case, and that's going to take time. Best to start now.

The bottom line here is that you don't want your main source of income to be dependent on your ability to exchange your time and labor for money. Otherwise, when situations occur that prevent you from making money in that way, usually you're the one who is out of luck. Instead, you want to create and/or own assets that generate money without you having to sacrifice 8 hours of your life and energy for it every day.

You must stop thinking that the only way to make money is by punching in and out at some job for a specific number of hours every week. You have to snap out of the lie that the only way to get paid is to wait for a meager paycheck from some employer every two weeks.

It can be very easy to miss the importance of this point when our culture has been brainwashed to think that our current understanding of "work" is *normal and healthy*. It's not normal. It's not healthy. It's insane. It's predatory. It's not sustainable. It takes advantage of people who don't understand the value that they bring to the table and keeps a tiny handful of opportunistic people exorbitantly wealthy and powerful because so many believe that there is no other way.

Slow down and meditate on what I'm about to say here: *nobody really likes this system except for the people at the top of the food chain who are reaping all of the staggering profits from your labor, your ideas, your energy, and your time.*

We can and we must do better. YOU can do better.

In your quest for riches and success, don't lose your soul in the process. Don't buy the lie that money is the root of all evil. It isn't. Money just amplifies who you already are...and you get to choose who that is and what that looks like for you.

What if you figured out how to make something that got you paid every week, every day or even every hour? How would that change things for you and your loved ones? What kind of freedom would that bring you?

More importantly, what kind of person will you be with that kind of freedom?

If you are going to do any kind of creative work on your own, there WILL be people who look to you as a leader, so let's talk about that for a moment.

Leadership is an intense responsibility and it can feel really scary – but it doesn't have to be if you just remember the Golden Rule and treat others the way you would want to be treated. Basically, don't be a selfish, greedy jerk. There is more than enough for everyone and self-absorbed narcissists make terrible leaders.

Good leaders calm people down and speak in terms of actual, practical solutions to the problems that a group is facing. They take ownership of the problems at hand and actively work on collaborating with people – even those they might disagree with – to solve the challenges ahead. Good leaders demonstrate compassion, integrity, hope, love, character, empathy, and are the kinds of people you know would always put their needs behind the needs of the group. They're the kinds of people who pull over to help you change a blown tire if you are stranded on the side of the road. Good leaders are willing to put themselves on the line and serve even when times are tough because it's the right thing to do. Good leaders don't need the approval of others or care about "winning," and in many cases are happy to let someone else take the credit for something because they are secure in their own identity.

Put simply: Good leaders bring people together and solve problems with empathy, innovation, and creativity. They care more about people than profit. Humble but confident creators who have devoted themselves to a cause bigger than themselves make good leaders. Surround yourself with them and do as they do.

On the other hand, bad leaders rile people up and constantly speak in angry, finger-pointing rhetoric while not actually offering tangible solutions. They deflect any responsibility for their role in the failures of the group. Their entire mode of operation is based around getting anyone who will listen to think that the cause of all problems lay squarely on the shoulders of someone else. That could mean a different political party, religious *(or non-religious)* group, a different race, other coworkers, and basically anyone *but themselves*. They seem almost completely incapable of taking responsibility for anything that could be perceived in any way as negative, and they never seem to be able to sincerely apologize for any wrong that their actions or inactions have caused others. Bad leaders take credit for things they didn't actually have anything to do with and constantly need the approval of others because they're secretly insecure. They function primarily on the competitive plane and only care about the appearance of "winning" or being "the best" at something. Additionally, bad leaders can never say anything good about those they might disagree with.

Put simply: Bad leaders push people apart and create more problems than they solve by projecting their anger, insecurities, and fear onto others. They care more about power, profit, and control than people. Manipulative, boastful, arrogant and self-centered narcissists do not make good leaders. Steer clear and avoid them.

If you don't understand this, it is very easy to get caught up in the noise of the mass-media-manufactured outrage tornado that makes its money by constantly spreading anger, gossip, drama, and fear. These outlets for some reason continue to uphold the age-old moniker of "if it bleeds, it leads" and every day seem to have some example of terrible leadership to keep you distracted with. We all slip up and can exhibit good and bad qualities sometimes, but *which do you practice?*

There are a small handful of people who would be very pleased if you would just stop thinking about all of this right now. In fact, your current employer might be one of those people. I hope not, but if they are, they'd be overjoyed if you would forever remain a quiet, obedient employee who never asks questions or expects a raise or better treatment. They'd love it if you never talked about your salary with your co-workers. They'd *really* love it if you never even think that you could do better for yourself somewhere else...*but you can.*

They'd appreciate nothing more than you just doing what you are told and falling in line. They want you to think that you must stay dependent on them for a mediocre paycheck that you've convinced yourself is good enough...even though they may be pulling in billions in profits. People like this do not actually care about you. They only care about themselves. What they don't want you to realize is that *their extreme wealth is dependent on you and what you do...or don't do.*

Work *can* be a symbiotic and mutually beneficial relationship. If you have one of those kinds of jobs, then great! You are among a lucky few. If you actually enjoy your job and are treated well by your employer, that's awesome and I am happy for you. However, that still does not change my suggestion to figure out ways to create multiple streams of income for yourself. Why *wouldn't* you want assets that generate money without you having to trade your time and labor for it?

Let me be very clear: if your current situation is not good, you need to figure out your exit strategy, confront it, or change something ASAP. If you and enough of your coworkers refuse to put up with that kind of nonsense, they'll either have to improve the working conditions for you or they'll eventually go out of business. You have options. Lots of them. Don't believe the lie that you don't.

If you know things aren't going to get better but do nothing about it, you are the one holding yourself back from a better life by your inaction.

Again, you must abandon the idea that you can achieve true financial independence if you just *"pull yourself up by your bootstraps"* and work really hard for someone else for 40+ years of your life. Sure, you might get some half-hour breaks and a handful of vacation or sick days sprinkled in along the way. Maybe if you're lucky, you'll get some healthcare benefits and a few days off if you have a kid or if a family member dies. And hey, when a global pandemic devastates the global economy with record high levels of unemployment, they might toss you a few extra bucks an hour and call it "hero pay." *Oh, how kind of them!* Thanks but no thanks.

I don't know about you, but it sure seemed to me like the way our collective "work culture" handled the pandemic was overall pretty terrible.

Especially for those who suddenly found themselves being called "essential workers" all over the place. In many cases, this was just a fancy of way of saying, *"Hey, so unfortunately you can't work from home due to the crappy nature of your job and well...we kinda need you to keep doing that job because otherwise these supply chains and systems will collapse entirely...so, buck up soldier! Make sure to take your vitamin C and wear that mask snugly around your mouth and nose while you're dealing with all those belligerent customers!"*

Throw in the fact that the US is currently one of the only countries in the world where people's healthcare is tied to their jobs and you've got yourself a recipe for disaster. What do you think happens when people lose those jobs during a global health crisis? Uh-oh! No more healthcare either! If you are one of the lucky ones who has never had to worry about how you're going to pay for something as important as your healthcare, then congratulations...but that is not the reality for a very large segment of the population of the US at the time of this writing. There are amazing and dedicated people around the country who are working to change that – but until then, whether I like it or not – having financial independence and reliable income makes navigating big problems like this a lot less stressful. You can do that by leveraging your creativity into building and owning assets so that when the storms of life hit, you are better prepared to handle them.

As I've mentioned, I have had some very significant health challenges in my close family over the years and my fair share of them as well. I know what it's like to avoid going to the doctor or seeing a professional when you need help because you have no idea how you are going to pay for it.

I for one am all for robust societal safety nets that exist to help struggling people and families. I have been there and am eternally grateful for the people who daily work to help those in need. For some people, it's the only way they can afford basic necessities. Never feel ashamed to get the kind of help you need if you really need it. Don't listen to anyone who says otherwise. Their calloused opinions don't matter. Also, if you are one of those people who works to ensure that people can get the help they need regardless of how much cash they have in the bank, thank you. You are quite literally saving and changing lives for the better.

Making money in the creative way is all about adding value to the world around you with intention and empathy. Wealth is attracted to confidence in your craft.

Don't sabotage your creative efforts by stressing yourself out to try and make things for the sole purpose of turning a profit. Make things for the joy of making things and getting better at your craft. The money and opportunities will follow eventually, and often they come from the most unexpected places and at the most unexpected times. At least that has consistently been the case for me. I was offered a publishing deal during one of the biggest economic downturns in human history. Sure, I'd been writing and publishing my work online for well over a decade by this point, but that's just it: I wasn't even *thinking* about trying to get "picked" by some outside source to validate my work. I chose to write and publish consistently over time because I believed in what I was sharing and doing. I knew from studying those who have gone before me that this was the way forward to the kind of financial freedom I was seeking.

You waste your focus and energy by worrying about results, accolades, profit, fame, and what the majority of the world defines as "successful." You delay the manifestation of your goals by focusing on big, public wins and outside recognition. Focus on your daily practice and cultivating what you already have. Things have a funny way of working out when you do this.

I hope as we come to a close here that by now you have established it firmly in your mind that true success is something only you can define for yourself. Your work is to keep building and to do everything you can to prepare to receive the fruit of your labor when the time comes to harvest it as we discussed earlier.

That could be in ten years or it could be in ten days. It will be different for everyone. Just know that the moment you begin to hurry and try to climb some nebulous, undefined ladder or achieve some kind of "status" that you have slipped once more into the competitive mindset. This actually slows you down from achieving the things you think you want. So stop it!

Create, don't compete. You must choose to believe in yourself and your craft long before anyone else will.

Everything that I've shared so far about this journey and the challenges of publishing the new edition is to give you context for what it took for me to get this thing out into the world. What really is fascinating to me though was the timing of it all and how it got started. Since I have been writing pretty much every day for years, I can look back through old journal entries and remember what I was going through and when. I can see patterns emerge in my writing as I wrestle with the struggles of life on the blank page and my attempts to work through solving the problems I am facing *(as well as which ones I'm avoiding)*.

The blank page beckons our imagination. It is formless and full of untapped possibility.

It is an invitation to mine the depths of who we are, what we believe, and why. This is also the reason so many avoid filling the blank page. We are all secretly afraid of what we might find there...but we don't have to be. You may just find what you've been looking for all along. As author Julia Cameron says in her brilliant and life-changing book *The Artist's Way*, writing every day helps you hear yourself think. She says, "It is very difficult to complain about a situation morning after morning and month after month without being moved to constructive action." I'd been complaining about how much I couldn't stand doing design-for-hire work for *years* in my journals, but at the end of the day, I had just been too afraid to step away from something that had become so familiar. It felt like something I *had* to do simply because I knew *how* to do it and because I had been doing it for so long.

I finally got to a point where I could no longer avoid what was right there in dozens *(if not hundreds)* of journal entries: **I needed to let it go because it wasn't working and I was miserable.** This realization terrified me.

On top of that, I knew that my stressful full-time job wasn't working for me anymore either. My journal entries could attest to that, too. I finally opened up to the idea that I would focus on finishing this book and taking a better opportunity if it came along. This idea terrified me as well, but it's funny how things work out sometimes. Shortly before publishing this edition, just such an opportunity did arrive. It was very unexpected, very timely, and it was an offer that I would have been foolish to turn down. It has been such a breath of fresh air and I am incredibly grateful. The details aren't important, but I will say that the new job gave me the freedom and focus to be able to finish this manuscript by my deadline, along with a substantial pay raise, a more rewarding working environment, and a paid sabbatical week off every six weeks. At the time of this writing, building so much intentional time for rest and creativity into a work culture is almost completely unheard of. I aim to change that...but that's another story for another time.

Maybe you're thinking about a particular situation right now and wondering if you need to let go of something that isn't working anymore *(or maybe never did in the first place)*. I can make no specific guarantees, but if any of this is resonating with you and you feel that uneasy lurch in your stomach at the thought of finally freeing yourself of whatever you're struggling with, chances are high that you should pay attention to that feeling. Take the leap and get out of whatever it is you're doing or tolerating that is continually leaving you miserable. Choose to believe in yourself and your creativity. Things will eventually open up for you that would not happen otherwise. I mean really, what do you have to lose by trying?

I mentioned earlier that the day after sharing a photo of the self-published edition of my book was when I was offered the publishing deal to create this one. *What I **didn't** mention* was that the offer was extended quite literally the day after we decided to wind down our design agency. I only know this because I have the journal entries to prove it.

Coincidence? Maybe. Maybe not...but I was certainly freaked out!

I have way too many questions about our strange shared existence and have had my fair share of weird "woo-woo" experiences, but this one shook me a bit.

I had yet to tell anyone publicly that we were winding down our business and I had dealt with so much mental noise over marketing the self-published edition. There was so much of that noise that I pretty much didn't market it at all.

I was afraid people would think I was being arrogant or self-centered by promoting a book about getting rich when so many were struggling...even though I knew that the content in it would help those very same people! None of this was useful for me at the time of course, but at least now I can remind you that the noise and the fear in your head is not unique...*and that you can beat it.* I don't understand the specifics of *how* the timing of this particular book deal worked out, but part of me likes to think that somewhere in the vast expanse of this fascinating, terrifying, bizarre, beautiful, chaotic, weird and wonderful existence that somebody is out there cheering on us "creative types." Maybe it was God or the Universe or the Great Creator or the "Formless Substance"...or heck, maybe it was Wallace Wattles himself sending me a wink from somewhere out in the cosmos, another dimension, or the ether. I have no idea and I've stopped trying to figure it all out. Doing so is a waste of time and energy and will always be up for debate...and I'm not interested in those debates anymore. My hope is simply that I have maintained the spirit and intention of the original author with this new edition – which I believe is to help people just like you get rich with your creativity while also realizing the riches you have already. *This one's for you, Wallace!*

You will never know exactly how any of this will play out. Keep creating anyway and focus on what really matters.

I am sure that there are all kinds of things that haven't worked out the way you thought they would. Everyone has those experiences. The difference maker is in what you choose to do next. Do you use those perceived failures as fuel for your creativity...or do you let them keep you stuck in self-loathing, mental time travel, and depression? You see, life often takes sudden and serendipitous turns for those who have chosen the creative path over the competitive one. When the only person you're competing with and trying to be better than is the person you were yesterday, your life will start to look a whole lot different. You just never know who will be impacted by something you made years ago or the opportunities that will open up for you over time.

If you keep creating even when you aren't making money on those creations, you are truly free to make what you want and find your voice. Chances are really, *really* small that you're going to suddenly generate any kind of substantial income from your creative work or new business endeavors for quite awhile.

Like, chances of you winning the lottery 47 times in a row while getting struck by lightning each time kind of small. **That's normal and that's okay.** Expect this to be the case. If you mentally prepare yourself for this fact here and now, it becomes much easier to stop worrying about how long something is going to take and **focus on what actually matters: your dedication to keep creating anyway.**

You can never know for sure how long achieving your goals will take. Do your best and work at them daily. Stop focusing on results and focus on trusting the process and the practice.

If I had not done the work of self-publishing the first edition a few years ago, I wouldn't have been able to do those giveaways because I wouldn't have had a book to give away in the first place. If I hadn't *announced* those giveaways, the publisher *(who I was connected with on social media)* would not have seen the book, and thus would not have offered me the deal. Additionally, if I hadn't gone to an author's business conference ten years earlier *where I met this publisher and learned all about publishing books,* I wouldn't have been connected with him on social media. Oh, and if I hadn't decided to start my own business prior to attending that conference, I would have had no reason to go to it, and thus wouldn't have even met him. On and on it goes. I'm sure you can trace similar paths to where you are now by looking back a bit.

The question is: do you see it yet?

Do you see that this *"getting rich in the certain way"* thing will *never* be about doing so quickly, but instead is about the countless daily decisions that you make over the course of your life and career? Do you see that the idea of "getting rich quick" is a fantasy? *(Unless of course you were born with rich parents or suddenly receive a financial windfall from an inheritance or the lottery)* Don't leave your wealth and future success up to chance. Get rich with intention and empathy. Get rich with the scientific, creative and "certain way." It is much more fulfilling and sustainable over the long haul.

Your life and the things in it today are fruit from the seeds of action, intention, attention, and perspective that you planted yesterday.

You can learn a lot about yourself and the way the world works by gardening. Years ago, I started gardening as a way to process and attempt to heal from a significant amount of traumatic life experiences that my family and I have endured over the years. One of the things you can learn when gardening is how much of what we say, do, think, and believe can be compared to seeds that we plant in our lives. If you constantly tell yourself that you're never going to have a better life or that you're just a huge screw up, chances are high that you will act accordingly and reap the fruit of those actions and thoughts. On the contrary, if you start changing those narratives in your head, you eventually will start acting differently and reap better results. The kinds of "seeds" you plant today matter because they will determine the harvest you reap tomorrow. You must cut out and cut off the things that choke the life out of whatever it is that you are trying to grow. You must actively choose to fill your imagination with possibility, hope, peace, and creativity. Avoid filling it with fear, negativity, anger, despair, and hopelessness. You must remain present while still planning, planting, and building for a better future instead of simply wishing you were somewhere else.

As James Oppenheim said, "The foolish person seeks happiness in the distance. The wise person grows it under their feet." Put another way, beauty, riches, and abundance grow where you plant and cultivate them. If I can turn a crappy back patio into a small home-grown sanctuary, so can you. If I can learn to start and run a business, so can you. If I can learn to play guitar and piano and how to compose and release music albums, so can you. If I can leave crappy jobs for better ones, so can you. If I can cut toxic people out of my life, so can you. If I can write and self-publish a book that goes on to get picked up by a bigger publisher later, so can you. If I can go from being broke to being rich, so can you. **If I can manifest and monetize my ideas, so can you.**

The overall message of this book is pretty simple: you can get rich and enjoy your life if you put in the work every day to get there.

What, were you hoping for something else? Sorry, champ! Nobody is going to do this stuff for you! You must choose yourself. If you lean into your creativity, you can develop and benefit from your ideas, start your own business endeavors, and CREATE wealth for yourself and your loved ones instead of always hustling for that next paycheck or always depending on an employer.

Work at your goals every single day. Write them down somewhere that you can see them regularly. If you haven't taken any practical action since you started reading this, there's no time like the present to do so. Now is the only time you ever have, so don't waste it. Make that vision board. Surround yourself with people of like-mind who are pursuing similar goals. Avoid hanging around negative and pessimistic people. They will only drag you down. Stop wasting your life getting sucked into the outrage tornado of media-manufactured societal, political, and class divisions, status games, and the mindless consumption of mental garbage.

Stop scrolling and go make something. Defy the distractions and fears in your head and focus on building something that only you can build. I obviously cannot make any specific claims as to how much money you will generate since everyone is different and each situation varies based on a wide array of factors. What I can say for certain is that you have all kinds of great ideas that can lead to creating an amazing life for yourself. You just need to put in the work to build it. You've already taken *at least* the first step by reading this book. A decision like that is the starting point. Congratulations, my friend. You have taken a big and important step. We have now come full circle to a game I invited you to play when we first got started on this journey together. It was an invitation you agreed to accept. So take a look around at how far you've come, even just with the way you see the world now. I'm proud of you. Give yourself credit for committing to the journey as well as the path ahead. You are the one who gets to decide what that looks like.

You must choose to build a life you don't want to escape from. Start now and begin to improve your existing environment however you can, one piece, one step, one rep, and one day at a time.

You can live a life that is far more exciting and fulfilling than taking orders all day sitting in a cubicle or working some crap low-paying job for a boss you can't stand with people you don't like. You can build that creative studio that you dream of, step by step and piece by piece. You can learn that instrument or develop that skill. You can move out of that city. You can make more than enough money than you know what to do with. You can get out of that toxic relationship or situation or workplace and find or develop better ones. You can reinvent yourself and be the person you really want to be. You've just got to make the choice to stop waiting around, put in the work, and make it happen. No one else is going to do it for you.

I know that some of this may feel repetitive - that is intentional. Your mind works like a muscle, and if you want to be strong you've got to get those reps in, champ.

I repeat these concepts again and again because we've been so bombarded with various forms of nonsense, advertising, and empty promises since we showed up on this floating blue rock. It can feel almost impossible to hear the signal through the noise. Don't listen to the "experts" who insist you have to go through them before you can create what you want to create. Don't listen to those who say you aren't good enough yet or that you have to wait for someone else to choose you for some winning team. **They're wrong. Start learning now and keep building.**

Beware the notion that you need to wait for some glorious glowing sign in the heavens *before* you are ready to get started in the pursuit of a better life. It's time to get started NOW. This isn't about chance or luck. What I am telling you and have shared throughout this book works. It does not matter what kinds of challenges you face. The principles that Wallace and I have presented here can be applied to every area of your life, regardless of your current education, economic status, reputation, race, religious or political beliefs, gender, sexual orientation, location, or age. **Creativity transcends all of that.** So what are you waiting for – *another* invitation? You've already got one, friend. Time to get on with it already!

You are ready now. Creativity always starts out messy. Get moving, keep learning, and keep building every day.

The happiest and wealthiest people in the world don't become that way by accident or by trying to reach the top of some never-ending corporate ladder. They become that way on purpose. They do so by bringing their own creative ideas to life. They take action daily to manifest them. They work at and refine them until they reach their goals. They push through pain, fear, anger, regret, frustration, depression, uncertainty, disappointment, anxiety, loss, grief, betrayal, trauma, and tragedy. They choose love. Happy and wealthy people choose to focus on the good things in life and are thankful for what they have. They choose to meditate on what they can do, not what they can't do. They choose to learn, practice, and master useful skills that help them live meaningful, abundant, creative lives. **You can do the same.**

Do what you can with what you have right where you are. Stay present, stay thankful, and avoid the distractions that this world throws at you.

I wish you joy, peace, abundance, more wealth and ideas than you know what to do with, and the wisdom and integrity to use it all for good. More than that, may you find your voice, happiness, love, hope, and contentment in the process. There are additional resources in the pages ahead that will help you further in your quest for success if you aren't sure where to go or what to do next. You just never know what opportunities are waiting for you right around the corner if you connect with the right people or actually lean in and learn to do that thing you've always wanted to do. Decide to be the type of person who stops waiting around for someone else to "pick" you. You don't need their approval. **You are good enough.**

You can do this. Now go get started. Rise up - go make something, and be excellent to each other!

The process of manifesting and monetizing your ideas takes time. It takes practice. It takes patience. It takes perseverance, grit, and more trial and error than you ever think it will when you first get started. But it works...*and it's worth it.* If you put in the work and create something of value, you can and *should* learn how to profit from it. My hope is that this book will continue to help you on that journey long after you have finished reading it for the first time. I believe in you. Believe in yourself and don't make any of what you have learned here more complicated than it actually is. After all – this isn't rocket science, my friend.

This is the science of getting rich.

- Ryan J. Rhoades
May, 2021

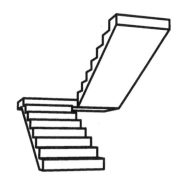

Faith is taking the first step even when you don't see the whole staircase.

- Dr. Martin Luther King, Jr. -

recommended reading

"Great leaders create opportunities that equip and mobilize others. They don't just grow leaders, they multiply them."
- Steve Addison

"In a time of drastic change, it is the learners who inherit the future. The learned find themselves equipped to live in a world that no longer exists."
- Eric Hoffer

I figure it's much easier to learn from those who have gone before me than it is to reinvent the wheel. Books help with stuff like that. In school, reading books was often a horrible, agitating chore that we had to do in order to pass a test or write a paper. You've got to get over that mentality if you want to really take your life, your creativity, and your business endeavors to the next level. Some of the wealthiest and smartest people in the world have taken the time to invest in anyone who is willing to listen by writing books. Oftentimes they are available for free at your local library or for less than $20 apiece online or in a local book store. You can only learn so much from the seemingly endless supply of click bait and 24/7 news cycle drama these days, and your information retention level *(that is, how much of what you read that you remember)* will be much higher if you don't have obnoxious advertisements and doom-and-gloom interrupting your train of thought every thirteen seconds. You won't have that problem with books.

Those listed here are all books I have benefited from personally in one way or another. Most I have read the whole way through, and some I use more like reference manuals that I revisit regularly. You will find patterns in them as you read and see that much of this creative journey is about cultivating your mindset and the regular practice of your craft – not obsessing over status, tools, or mastery of specific or antiquated techniques. You also most likely will find that trying to keep up with the monstrosity of what "social" and corporate media has become is not only a huge waste of time, focus, and energy – but also that your emotional, mental, and physical health will improve dramatically when you don't spend so much time *(or any time at all)* consuming it. You must tune it all out to tune into yourself.

As author Tim Ferriss says:

"Once you realize you can turn off the noise without the world ending, you are liberated in a way that few people know."

I have found this to be the case for me. Do you think I would have ever been able to finish this book while checking my phone every ten minutes or if I spent my whole day binging on Netflix or some other streaming video service? Think again. Every time you get that itch to pick up your phone and scroll through all the latest gossip, posturing, or drama going on, just keep in mind that you're encouraging them to keep pumping that crap out. Your attention is how they make their money. Stop it! Pick a random book from this list and read that instead, or go back and revisit this one. You have chosen to become a life-long learner. This is the way. ;)

Most of "real life" isn't like school, my friend. At least not yet. There are no standardized tests and nobody is telling you what books to read on this journey. You get to choose! My advice is simply this: pursue and learn about things that you enjoy and that you find yourself getting immersed in and losing track of time. Eventually if you want to, you can figure how to monetize those passions.

Do what you love and what leaves the world at least a little bit better than you found it. Work with people who are doing what you believe in. Learn from those who you look up to. Ask lots of questions and read a lot of books. Most people are often more willing to share the lessons they've learned along the way than you may think. You have literally nothing to lose and everything to gain.

Go get it, champ.

recommended reading

Stop Wasting Time & Burning Money
by Ryan J. Rhoades & Lany Sullivan

The Artist's Way & Finding Water
by Julia Cameron

The Soul of Money
by Lynne Twist

Think Again
by Adam Grant

The E-Myth Revisited
by Michael Gerber

Think and Grow Rich
& The Law of Success
by Napoleon Hill

The War of Art, Turning Pro,
Gates of Fire, & The Artist's Journey
by Steven Pressfield

Rework
by Jason Fried & David
Heinemeier Hansson

How to Think Like Leonardo da Vinci
by Michael J. Gelb

How to Win Friends
and Influence People
by Dale Carnegie

Striking Thoughts
by Bruce Lee

Damn Good Advice
by George Lois

Love Yourself Like Your Life
Depends on It & Rebirth
by Kamal Ravikant

The Almanack of Naval Ravikant
by Eric Jorgenson

Tools of Titans, Tribe of Mentors,
The Four Hour Workweek,
The Four Hour Chef, &
The Four Hour Body
by Tim Ferriss

The Practice, This is Marketing,
The Dip, Tribes, Purple Cow,
Linchpin, Poke the Box, &
The Icarus Deception
by Seth Godin

Choose Yourself, Reinvent Yourself,
The Power of No, & Skip the Line
by James Altucher

Steal Like an Artist,
Show Your Work,
& Keep Going
by Austin Kleon

Mastery & The Laws of Human Nature
by Robert Greene

The Obstacle is the Way, Ego is
the Enemy, Stillness is the Key,
Lives of the Stoics, The Daily Stoic,
Perennial Seller, & Trust Me,
I'm Lying: Confessions
of a Media Manipulator
by Ryan Holiday

recommended reading

The Millionaire Messenger, The Charge,
Life's Golden Ticket, High Performance
Habits, & The Motivation Manifesto
by Brendon Burchard

I Will Teach You To Be Rich
by Ramit Sethi

7 Habits of Highly Effective People
by Steven Covey

The Rise of the Creative Class
by Richard Florida

Delivering Happiness
by Tony Hsieh

Brainshare
by Joe Siecinski

Rising Strong, Dare to Lead,
& The Gifts of Imperfection
by Brené Brown

Big Magic
by Elizabeth Gilbert

The Magic of Thinking Big
by David J. Schwartz, Ph.D.

Mindfulness for Beginners
by Jon Kabat-Zinn

The Last Lecture
by Randy Pausch

Developing the Leader Within You
by John C. Maxwell

Thinkertoys &
Creative Thinkering
by Michael Michalko

Built to Sell &
The Automatic Customer
by John Warrillow

Start With Why, Leaders Eat
Last, & The Infinite Game
by Simon Sinek

The Meditations of Marcus Aurelius
& The Manual of Epictetus
translated by Sam Torode

Ogilvy on Advertising
by David Ogilvy

Guerrilla Marketing
by Jay Conrad Levinson

Don't Worry: Make Money &
Don't Sweat the Small Stuff
by Richard Carlson

Strengths Finder 2.0
by Tom Rath

The Success Principles
by Jack Canfield

The Suble Art of Not Giving a F*ck
by Mark Manson

Play It Away: A Workaholic's
Cure for Anxiety
by Charlie Hoehn

recommended reading

The Leader Phrase Book
by Patrick Alain

Atomic Habits
by James Clear

The Power of Full Engagement
by Jim Loehr and Tony Schwartz

Blue Ocean Strategy & Blue Ocean Shift
by W. Chan Kim &
Renée A. Mauborgne

The Lean Startup
by Eric Ries

The Starfish and the Spider
by Ori Brafman & Rod Beckstrom

The Life Changing Magic of Tidying Up
by Marie Kondo

The Art of Peace
by Morihei Ueshiba and John Stevens

Book Yourself Solid
by Michael Port

The Cosmic Journal
by Yanik Silver

ABC's of Conscious Capitalism
by Laura Hall & Brent Metcalf

Flow: The Psychology
of Optimal Experience
by Mihaly Csikszentmihalyi

The Hero with a Thousand Faces
by Joseph Campbell

The Writer's Journey
by Christopher Vogler

The World as I See It &
Out of My Later Years
by Albert Einstein

Mastery: The Keys to Success &
Long-Term Fulfillment
by George Leonard

The Richest Man Who Ever Lived
by Steven K. Scott

The Power of Patience
by M.J. Ryan

Awareness
by Anthony de Mello

Ignore Everybody &
39 Other Keys to Creativity
by Hugh MacLeod

This is Your Brain on Music
by Daniel J. Levitin

Unlimited Power
by Tony Robbins

Profit First
by Mike Michalowicz

You Are a Badass at Making Money
by Jen Sincero

recommended reading

The Alchemist
by Paulo Coelho

Fahrenheit 451
by Ray Bradbury

1984
by George Orwell

The Hunger Games Trilogy
by Suzanne Collins

Ready Player One
by Ernest Cline

The Hobbit &
The Lord of the Rings Trilogy
by J.R.R. Tolkien

The Time Keeper &
Tuesdays with Morrie
by Mitch Albom

The Butterfly Effect, The Noticer,
& The Noticer Returns
by Andy Andrews

Ishmael
by Daniel Quinn

The Harry Potter Series
by J.K. Rowling

The Greatest Salesman in the World
by Og Mandino

Joshua
by Joseph Girzone

Caste: The Origins
of Our Discontents
by Isabel Wilkerson

Psycho-Cybernetics
by Maxwell Maltz

Limitless
by Jim Kwik

No Rules Rules: Netflix &
The Culture of Reinvention
by Reed Hastings & Erin Meyer

From Me to You:
by Dotun Fadairo

Rest: Why You Get More Done
When You Work Less
by Alex Soojung-Kim Pang

Superbetter
by Jane McGonigal

Change Your World
by Michael Ungar, PhD

Wreck This Journal
by Keri Smith

You Are the Placebo
by Dr. Joe Dispenza

Everything is Spiritual
by Rob Bell

Deep Work & Digital Minimalism
by Cal Newport

recommended reading

Multipliers: How the Best
Leaders Make Everyone Smarter
by Liz Wiseman

The 22 Immutable Laws of Marketing
by Al Ries and Jack Trout

Killing Giants
by Stephen Denny

Healing Trauma
by Peter A. Levine Ph.D.

Loonshots
by Safi Bahcall

Jab, Jab, Jab, Right Hook
by Gary Vaynerchuk

Superforecasting
by Philip Tetlock & Dan Gardner

Embrace Your Weird
by Felicia Day

The Righteous Mind: Why Good People
Are Divided by Politics and Religion
by Jonathan Haidt

The True Believer
by Eric Hoffer

The Revolution Generation
by Josh Tickell

Extreme Ownership &
Discipline Equals Freedom
by Jocko Willink

The Tipping Point & Outliers
by Malcolm Gladwell

The Art of Learning
by Josh Waitzkin

Getting Everything You Can
Out of All You've Got
by Jay Abraham

The Creative Cure
by Jacob Nordby

The Power of Full Engagement
by Jim Loehr & Tony Schwartz

Leadership and Self-Deception
by The Arbinger Institute

Debt: The First 5,000 Years
by David Graeber

Finding God in the Waves:
How I Lost My Faith and Found It
Again Through Science
by Mike McHargue

Blue Like Jazz & Building a Storybrand
by Donald Miller

Man's Search for Meaning
by Viktor Frankl

The Choice: Embrace the Possible
by Dr. Edith Eva Eger

Cosmos
by Carl Sagan

additional resources & support

Your Local Small Business Development Center
www.sba.gov/tools/local-assistance/sbdc

Chances are high that you have a local Small Business Development Center near you. The SBDC gives free business advising and mentorship to pretty much anyone who wants it. They'll help you learn the art and nuances of running your own business endeavors. If the link above doesn't work, just search for SBDC. It's also a great place to meet other local business owners and build together.

StartupStash.com

This is a great site that is full of more resources than you will know what to do with. It is extremely well organized by a wide variety of topics. Stuff like marketing, design, software to use for pretty much anything you can think of, generating ideas, web hosting, etc. If you are building a business, bookmark this page.

1000 True Fans by Kevin Kelly
http://kk.org/thetechnium/1000-true-fans

"A true fan is defined as someone that will buy anything you produce," Kelly says. In the article he talks about how to go about forming an action plan for reaching those true fans and building a following, a product, and a business around it. This article is a quintessential read for anyone who wants to do anything "creative" for a living. You can also find videos on YouTube on the topic.

SCORE: Business Advising
www.score.org

SCORE's mission is to foster vibrant small business communities through mentorship and education. With the nation's largest network of volunteer, expert business mentors, SCORE has helped more than 11 million entrepreneurs since 1964.

additional resources & support

National Suicide Prevention Lifeline
1-800-273-8255
www.suicidepreventionlifeline.org

The Lifeline provides 24/7, free and confidential support for people in distress, prevention and crisis resources for you or your loved ones, and best practices for professionals. If you are worried you may harm yourself or someone else, please call. Really. You don't need to face the challenges that you are dealing with alone and your life matters. Yes, you can get better. You can start now. Give them a call.

Social Services
HHS.gov

Find out how to get temporary assistance in your state if you are struggling with low-income and are trying to figure out how to keep food on the table. The people who work in social services have devoted their lives to helping people get back on their feet. There is no shame in asking for help. It is there for you when you need it.

Khan Academy
www.khanacademy.org

The Khan Academy was founded by educator Salman Khan in 2006 as a non-profit educational organization dedicated to providing online tutoring and learning services to users across a wide variety of topics. I can't recommend this site highly enough if you are wanting to learn just about anything. Did I mention it's free?

Masterclass.com

Want to learn how to compose music with Hans Zimmer, shoot hoops with Steph Curry, or shred on the guitar like Carlos Santana? Whatever you are interested in, you can learn a lot from the masters at Masterclass.com. This is a paid subscription service but I have found it to be one of the best investments I've ever made.

additional resources & support

Gumroad.com

Gumroad is an easy to use but powerful e-commerce platform that makes it easy for creators to get paid for their work. You can use it to sell online courses, artwork, products, or anything else that you make. You don't need expensive software or website builders to sell something online and you can start today with Gumroad.

Shopify.com

For a more robust e-commerce solution, Shopify is one of the best out there. We use Shopify to host our online store *(RDShop.biz)* and connect it to Printful (mentioned below). There is a yearly subscription fee but in my experience, it is well worth the investment to have such a powerful software at your fingertips.

Printful
printful.reformdesigns.biz

Want to make and sell your own custom products? Printful makes it easy. With a wide and ever-increasing selection of new products to customize, sell, and integrate with the e-commerce platform of choice, Printful is an entrepreneurial artist's playground. If you sign up with the link above, I'll get a small bonus for referring you. If that link doesn't work for some reason, just check out printful.com

Patreon.com

Patreon makes it simple for creators of all types to build and connect with a supportive fan base. They make it easy to receive recurring donations from your biggest fans. This can be set up in all kinds of unique ways and you would do well to read through Patreon's blog to learn how some of their most successful creators are doing so. At the time of this writing, a good friend of mine has a Patreon following that sends him over $20,000 per MONTH for making YouTube videos and access to their growing community. **If they can do it, so can you.**

additional resources & support

The Noun Project
thenounproject.com

The Noun Project is a website that aggregates and catalogs symbols that are created and uploaded by graphic designers around the world. You can use it as a design resource for free or commercial projects if you buy the license. There's a great app to go with it that integrates with Adobe software or MacOS. If you liked a lot of the iconography throughout this book, you can thank The Noun Project artists.

Book Like a Boss
blab.reformdesigns.biz

If you're running any kind of business, the amount of time you waste trying to figure out when to connect with prospects or clients is enormous. Take the guesswork out of the equation and take control of your calendar. Book Like a Boss is hands-down my favorite appointment booking software. There are a lot of options for all kinds of different service providers as well as automation solutions for those of you who like making robots do the tedious stuff. If my affiliate link doesn't work, do a web search for Book Like a Boss.

Wordpress.com, Wix.com & Squarespace.com

If you are looking to build a website, there are a lot of places you can do so with relative ease these days. Thousands of free and paid templates are available through Wordpress, Wix, and Squarespace. You can build free sites through all of the above providers and upgrade later for more customization features if you choose to.

Zapier.com & IFTTT.com

Zapier and IFTTT (If This, Then That) are great software solutions for anyone who wants to automate the more tedious aspects of managing an online business. The possibilities are endless when you can get all of your apps to work together. There's a learning curve for sure, but they basically give you superpowers. ;)

A life lived for art
is never a life wasted.

- Ben Haggerty -

Moving Forward Decision Map

Event or situation

ASK YOURSELF:
Can I control this or do anything practical to improve upon it?

YES!

NOPE

Great! Do that.

Your energy and focus is best utilized when you are staying present in the moment and focused on creating, building, and moving forward in the realization of your goals. If you hear about events or situations that are beyond your control, the best thing to do is decide what you CAN do, and then choose to do that.

Change your focus.

The most effective use of your energy is when it is directed towards taking practical action. Sometimes that means doing nothing but changing your focus & what actions you take next because the things or events you are focused on are beyond your control. This is not sticking your head in the sand. This is the only way.

thank you's and acknowledgements

This book would not exist without the encouragement and support of more people than I can even begin to list.

Writing and publishing a book like this is a massive, exhausting endeavor and I am eternally grateful for all of those who have helped contribute to bringing this project to life. From the bottom of my heart, thank you. I hope you have enjoyed it.

First of all, to my wife – thank you for your continued love and companionship over the years as we have traveled this creative journey together. The best is yet to come and I would not be who I am without you. You truly are my best friend and I love you beyond words. Thank you for cheering me on through the finish line.

To my parents and my sisters – thank you for always encouraging me to pursue my dreams and my creativity, even when the road has been difficult at times. I love and appreciate you and can't wait to see what we keep building together.

To Brent, Nathan, and Daniel – thank you for your listening ear, your hopeful words, your strength, your humor, and your vision. You believed in me when I didn't believe in myself, and I cannot thank you enough for being such great and supportive friends. It's been a wild ride but you've made the journey worth taking.

To Sarah – thanks for your help with editing the original manuscript and the relentless motivation you have shared with us over the years to keep moving forward. It's been an honor to create and take on giants with you.

And of course, to you – If it weren't for the generosity, support, counsel, and kindness of people just like you, I would not have the opportunities that I do and I would not be where I am. There are so many people who have in various ways supported my family and I on this creative journey. I name some on the following page but there are so many more. Thank you for believing in us and the crazy idea that we can make the world better with creativity. Words don't do justice to the depth of gratitude I hold in my heart for you. My prayer is that this book has been a blessing to you and that it will be a welcome companion on your own creative path to success and a life that you love. Much love to you and yours.

thank you's and acknowledgements

In no particular order and for a whole variety of reasons, massive thanks go out to...

Wallace Wattles, Marissa Brassfield, Mona Holmes, Jo'el Adifon, Caleb New, Christian Erickson, Jim Kwik, Audrey Hagin, Brendon Burchard, Ramit Sethi, Steven Pressfield, Julia Cameron, James Altucher, Seth Godin, Steve Bremner, Jon Nori, Rodney Vance, Mark Houlihan, Kamal & Naval Ravikant, Rebecca Clayton, Melody Aldermann, Marcia Bagnall, the Salem SBDC, Eileen Casey White, Steve Bremner, Katie Freiling, Kyle Bowe, David Hancock, Rick and Robbie Frishman, Morgan James Publishing, Ryan Holiday, Austin Kleon, Sean & Laci McCabe, Sam Torode, Shashi Jain, David Graeber, Richard Florida, Rob Bell, Buckminster Fuller, Joe Siecinski, Tim Ferriss, Shyla Nelson Stewart, Bernie & Jane Sanders, Caleb & Jacob Wolcott, Dan Price, Lindsey Blackmore, Simon Baggerman, Cordell Winrow, Brandon Lee, Dennis and Sue Ellen Bontrager, Steven Delpino, Andrew Walsh, Jaren Barnes, Zara Altair, Cal Newport, Will Smith, Ira Glass, Brené Brown, Elizabeth Gilbert, Terry and Stacey Stibbards, Jayne Kim, Ki Chung, Christy Yom, Carol Shelton, Susan Richards, Ben Haggerty, Ryan Lewis, Nate Feuerstein, Lin-Manuel Miranda, Kim Leighty, Dan Piraro, Ricardo Perez, Tony Frazier, Cat Azevedo, Paul Carter, Hannah Starr, Quincy Washington, Rosa Oliver, Ben Northrop, Gregg Peterson, Kimberly Rugh, Laura Foley, Jeremy Clubb, Quinton and Deanna Markham, Kam Saar, Erin Braudrick and the rest of my old crew. Also, every author, artist or entrepreneur who has decided to challenge the status quo and build something better than they saw around them. You are loved and appreciated more than you know. I couldn't have done any of this without you.

To the rest of our brilliant creator friends, family, mentors, advisors, and fans – thank you. We love you. You are the reason we create. We believe in you and so appreciate all of your help and support over the years.

Now go forth and make something amazing!

See things clearly.

This is a simple world made complex
by the most mediocre of men.

You must be able to recognize what this
world is lacking - diagnose it - and then
find an elegant solution to make it better.
It's easier than you might think.

Clear your mind of everything except the
problem you are trying to solve, and then
visualize how to fix it. Truly see it with
your mind's eye.

Close your eyes and see it and you'll know:
Everything begins with an IDEA.
Everything begins with an IMAGE.
Once you have that, you BUILD.

- Jonathan Hickman -

If you have any questions, comments, or want some help bringing your own ideas to life, connect with me at ryanjrhoades.com

Thanks again for reading!

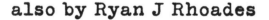

also by Ryan J Rhoades

Stop Wasting Time and Burning Money:
How to Crush Procrastination
& Live the Life of Your Dreams
(co-authored with Lany Sullivan)

The Absolute Essential Zombie Coloring Book
(co-created with Brent Metcalf)

Wallace D. Wattles

(1860 - 1911)

Wallace was an American author who has been widely quoted and cited as a source of insight, wealth, and inspiration by authors and leaders around the world. He grew up in Illinois. In addition to his writing, Wallace worked on a farm and fathered three children.

He was an avid writer and authored a number of books on a variety of topics pertaining to everyday life, health, and success. His writings encourage the reader to take responsibility for their own success and happiness by doing all they can in their immediate environment to practice gratitude while building the life they desire.

about the authors

Ryan J. Rhoades

Ryan is a prolific author, artist, and creator who loves bringing ideas to life and empowering others to do the same. He is the host of *The Creative Revolution Podcast*, where he interviews fascinating people about innovation, art, and making ideas happen in the 21st century. He started his first business in 2011. Some of Ryan's past clients include Marissa Brassfield, Jim Kwik, Jack Canfield, and Rick Frishman. He loves helping people unlock and unleash their creative superpowers. Ryan can currently be found making something somewhere in the Pacific Northwest, with plans to soon return home to Western Pennsylvania.

You can connect with him at
ryanjrhoades.com

Want to continue your Science of Getting Rich journey online?

visit ScienceOfGettingRich.info for resources, merch, updates and more!

notes & personal thoughts

notes & personal thoughts

notes & personal thoughts

notes & personal thoughts

notes & personal thoughts

notes & personal thoughts

A free ebook edition is available with the purchase of this book.

To claim your free ebook edition:

1. Visit MorganJamesBOGO.com
2. Sign your name CLEARLY in the space
3. Complete the form and submit a photo of the entire copyright page
4. You or your friend can download the ebook to your preferred device

Morgan James
BOGO™

A **FREE** ebook edition is available for you
or a friend with the purchase of this print book.

CLEARLY SIGN YOUR NAME ABOVE

Instructions to claim your free ebook edition:
1. Visit MorganJamesBOGO.com
2. Sign your name CLEARLY in the space above
3. Complete the form and submit a photo
   of this entire page
4. You or your friend can download the ebook
   to your preferred device

Print & Digital Together Forever.

Snap a photo   Free ebook   Read anywhere